DATE DUE

P9-APO-368

MAY 2 6 1988   BIRD   MAY 11 '88   RET

APR 1 8 1990   BIRD   APR 1 8 1990

MAY 24 1990   APR 30 1990 RET

A TIME FOR HYSTERIA

BY THE SAME AUTHOR:

The Quest for Peace

A TIME FOR HYSTERIA

The Citizen's Guide to Disarmament

by

Mortimer Lipsky

South Brunswick and New York:
A. S. Barnes and Company
London: Thomas Yoseloff Ltd

© 1969 by A. S. Barnes and Co., Inc.

Library of Congress Catalogue Card Number: 68-27228

A. S. Barnes and Co., Inc.
Cranbury, New Jersey 08512

Thomas Yoseloff Ltd
108 New Bond Street
London W. 1, England

SBN
498-06681-9
Printed in the United States of America

JX
1974
L565

Hp. 28.69

SO

To Anne

More precious than rubies

Acknowledgments

The author gratefully acknowledges permission to use selections from the following published material:

From *Fail-Safe*, by Eugene Burdick and Harvey Wheeler. Copyright 1962 by McGraw-Hill Company. Used by permission of McGraw-Hill Book Company.

From *On Thermonuclear War*, by Herman Kahn. Copyright 1961 by Princeton University Press. Used by permission of Princeton University Press.

From *The Rand Hymn*, words and music by Malvina Reynolds. Copyright 1961 by Schroder Music Co. (ASCAP). Used by permission. All rights reserved.

Contents

Contents

9

A TIME FOR HYSTERIA

If you wish to be brothers, let the arms fall from your hands. One cannot love while holding offensive arms.

POPE PAUL VI

1

A Time for Hysteria

This is a time for hysteria.

At this moment there is poised on Russian launching pads under earth and under water—on hair trigger alert and aimed at the United States—sufficient firepower to kill every American 145 times. At this moment there is poised on American launching pads under earth and under water—on hair trigger alert and aimed at the Soviet Union —sufficient firepower to kill every Russian 1,250 times.

We live in an apocalyptic age, when the daily press carries overtones of doomsday. Crisis follows on the heel of crisis and the lull between crises is a troubled truce filled with fears of war and preparations for war. The peoples of the world are weighted down with a foreboding dread of impending great and terrible events. Mankind has never been nearer to the fulfillment of that biblical curse, "They shall be burnt with hunger and devoured with burning heat and with bitter destruction." The phrase from the Bhagavad-Gita keeps recurring in

13

our minds, "I am become Death, the shatterer of worlds." To quote Congressman F. E. Hébert, an eyewitness to the first hydrogen bomb explosion at Eniwetok Atoll, "I had a feeling I was standing at the gates of hell, looking into eternity."

A Cassandra of doom is not needed to prophesy the fate of this bloodstained century. Listen to the voices of our leaders. At a press conference, on October 11, 1961, President Kennedy stated, "But we happen to live, because of the ingenuity of science and man's own inability to control his relationships one with another, we happen to live in the most dangerous time in the history of the human race."

The late President was reiterating the warning he had delivered before the United Nations General Assembly a few weeks earlier, on September 25, 1961: "Today, every inhabitant of this planet must contemplate the day when this planet may no longer be habitable. Every man, woman and child lives under a nuclear sword of Damocles, hanging by the slenderest of threads, capable of being cut at any moment by accident or miscalculation or by madness. The weapons of war must be abolished before they abolish us." He reiterated this dread on the eve of the Cuban confrontation: "The odds are at least even, if you think about it, on H-bomb war within ten years."

Listen to Sir Winston Churchill, who described our age as "a world of monstrous shadows moving in convulsive combinations through vistas of fathomless catastrophe."

An appeal addressed to the heads of states, on July 10, 1955, by nine of the world's outstanding scientists—Bertrand Russell, Percy W. Bridgman, Albert Einstein, Leopold Infeld, Hermann J. Muller, Cecil F. Powell, Joseph Rotblat, Hideki Yukawa and Frédéric Joliot-Curie — stressed that "we have found that the men who knew most are the most gloomy" about the future of the human race.

Listen to the experts: C. P. Snow believes that a nuclear blowup in the next ten years is a certainty. He said, "We know with the certainty of statistical truth that if enough of these weapons are made and by enough different states—some of them are going to blow up through accident, or folly, or madness—but the motives don't matter. What does matter is that the nature of the statistical fact is not a risk but a certainty."

Sir Bernard Lovell feels that the discussion of whether mankind might survive a nuclear war in the sixties is irrelevant because within ten to twenty years, at the most, the answer will be an unequivocal "No." Herman Kahn has a firm belief that we are not going to reach the year 2000—maybe not even the year 1975—without a cataclysm of some sort unless we do something about the present state of total peril.

Jerome B. Wiesner, scientific adviser to President Kennedy, writes, "There is every historical reason to conclude that, if we drift along as we are now doing, another major war will certainly occur." Professor William W. Kaufmann of the Massachusetts Institute of Technology states, "No high policy-maker can go for long under modern conditions without recognizing that a nuclear war could actually occur." Professor Harrison Brown sees a nuclear holocaust "almost certainly within the next century, quite possibly within the next twenty-five years."

Canada's Lieutenant General E. L. M. Burns declares,

"There is no end in sight except nuclear war" if the nuclear arms race proceeds and the guilty governments are "voting for nuclear war—nuclear war that may be decades away, but which will surely come."

Is this sense of panic and alarm warranted by the circumstances? Is this a time for horror type television political commercials showing a child picking petals on a daisy to the timing of a countdown which ends with a bomb explosion? After all, anxiety and imminent danger of death have been man's constant companions throughout history. The world has always been on the brink of war; during the last 400 years there has been an average of three wars every five years. Recorded history is a crescendo of mounting miseries accumulated from century to century: the Black Death, the Thirty Years War, the Nazi holocaust, the Soviet purges, Hiroshima, the Indian-Moslem communal slaughter, the Inquisition, the Japanese rape of China, the Mongol hordes—the list is endless. Somehow man has not only endured; he has prevailed.

In the past, no matter how terrible the disaster, mankind could not be killed. There could be confidence in the future, because in every calamity some would be spared. Destruction could never be more than fractional, limited, finite. In the past, there has always been a margin for human error. This margin now has been reduced, by the advances of science, to the narrowest of defiles: we no longer have room for trial and error or straying. Mr. Faulkner, the human race can in time recover from almost anything; but it cannot recover from universal death.

For the first time man now possesses the knowledge and the wherewithal to completely destroy all life on this planet. Whether or not this power will be used is another question: it exists. Nor would it avail aught to lament with Hesiod, "Would that I did not live in this time; would that I had died before or were born much later." We live in this time. Are we also to die in this time—suddenly, horribly, brutishly?

Listen to President Kennedy: "A full-scale nuclear exchange, lasting less than sixty minutes, could wipe out more than 300,000,000 Americans, Europeans and Russians, as well as untold numbers elsewhere." Listen to former United States Marine Commandant, General David M. Shoup: "when the nuclear exchange of the magnitude that is possible occurs, we will have not millions but 700 to 800 million dead." We would fall like summer flies; there would be no difference between the front and the rear, between soldiers and children. All would be incinerated. We would suffer 1,000 World War II's in one hour.

What are our elected leaders doing in the face of the greatest threat that has ever confronted the continued existence of man? They are busy feverishly piling megaton of destruction upon megaton—until the whole infernal heap teeters with a highly unstable imbalance. In their —and our—mindless horror, they have unleashed all the furies of a perverted science in a frenzied search for ever deadlier means of total annihilation. They—and we—have spent our national substance and sacrificed the better part of our energies, the sweat of our labor, the genius of our scientists, and the hopes of our children on preparations for wholesale human extermination. In the process, we have stolen from the hungry, the sick, the needy, the illiterate. We have, in the words of President Eisenhower, hung humanity from a cross of iron.

World expenditures of something like 130 billion dol-

lars a year have built a monstrous inflammable nuclear
stockpile of perhaps 350,000 megatons, awaiting only the
match to blow the entire earth sky-high. Nor are the
matches lacking. They are scattered all over the globe
and they are labelled Berlin, Laos, Vietnam, Korea, Kashmir, Cuba, Congo, Malaysia, Israel, Sikkim, Ladakh,
Cyprus, Taiwan, Quemoy, Matsu, Rann of Cutch. And
it takes only one match to light the fuse.

Thus, the chips pile up and the table stakes are raised
and raised again. In creating this mountain of mega-
death, our leaders have not safeguarded our security. Indeed, as President Kennedy pointed out, "in a spiraling
arms race a nation's security may be shrinking even as
its arms increase." The arms race between the United
States and the Soviet Union was best described by President Eisenhower as "two atomic colossi . . . doomed
malevolently to eye each other indefinitely across a trembling world." One inevitably calls to mind a painting by
Goya, at the Prado, depicting two men, sinking in quick-
sand, beating each other with clubs.

At the same time, our statesmen, as great political leaders who must appear as all things to all men, have not
ignored the universal yearning for peace. Continuous,
non-stop disarmament conferences have been in session
since the end of World War I—the longest-running show
on earth. For almost half a century our greatest minds
have devoted themselves unceasingly to a ritual pursuit
of disarmament. Yet all these efforts and all this striving
have achieved absolutely nothing. Not one arm, not one
cap pistol, not one slingshot, has been scrapped as a
result of almost fifty years of concentrated negotiations.

How was it possible for these mountains of pomp and

circumstance to heave and sweat so mightily and yet not bring forth even the tiniest mouse? It is inconceivable to the citizen that the heroic efforts of such lofty personages, over so many years, could result in such utter failure. Or, perhaps these diplomats did not fail after all. Perhaps they succeeded more handsomely than the citizen can understand. Perhaps it was their job to make certain that the negotiations did not result in the scrapping of any armaments. Perhaps the plenipotentiaries occupied their posts at the velvet-covered conference tables to make certain that the status quo was preserved and that the entrenched and vested interests of the military-industrial complex were not disturbed. Otherwise, how can we explain and understand the honors and accolades and tributes that have been accorded these public emissaries who have failed so miserably in the performance of their appointed tasks?

The first real glimmer of understanding of the problem of disarmament comes to the citizen when he understands that there is no real intent upon the part of his political and military leaders to achieve this professed goal. The alibis that the question of disarmament is highly technical, vast, immense, enormous, hopelessly complex, incredibly complicated—much too difficult for the ordinary citizen to grasp—are only smokescreens thrown up to obscure the real game being played behind the curtain.

It is a game of musical chairs, a quadrille, where each side takes turns in mouthing the same shopworn, insincere proposals as a sop to public opinion. First one side drags its feet; then the other. First one side comes forward with all sorts of enthusiastic ideas while the other holds back; then the roles are reversed. It is a puppet show performed in the grand manner to bemuse and beguile the country bumpkins—the humble citizenry, you and me. It offers the best of the Baird and Obraztsov companies, with the strings being pulled in Washington and Moscow. And woe betide the character who oversteps his appointed role. Off with his head: witness Lord Cecil and Harold Stassen.

How else can one interpret the chest thumping, the boastful braggadocio, the truculent browbeating, the scoring of debating points which constitute the parallel monologues that pass for negotiation in our time? Why should we then be surprised when these dialogues of the deaf fall on wooden ears? Actually, our leaders are afraid to negotiate in good faith because they are uncertain and insecure in their own positions and beliefs. They fear that if they ever sat down at the table with their opponents in a sincere effort to communicate like fellow human beings, the spectre of our enemy as Evil Incarnate—diabolical and unredeemed—that has so painfully been conjured up would vanish in thin air. What would the status of our political bureaucracy and of our military amount to if there were no enemy? Even more horrible: suppose sincere, good-faith negotiations showed some results?

The fact is that the real game of diplomacy is to probe the soft belly of the enemy in the first skirmishes of World War III. Analyze carefully (as we shall do) the proceedings at Geneva; scratch the surface of the draft resolutions put forth by either side. You will find that they are not designs for peace at all, but rather stratagems to outmaneuver the enemy and steal a march in the next war.

Surely nothing else can be expected from our diplomats and their negotiations. As creatures of our nation-state system, they carry to the disarmament table the precise attitudes which caused the Cold War and the arms race in the first place. The long drawn-out discussions on disarmament drag along as though we had a choice between war and peace. And very often the rapid rate of technological change has outstripped the glacier-slow pace of negotiation so that control plans change their very meaning even while they are being debated.

So this is the world picture at this writing: a mad headlong arms race in the laboratories and the missile works, and an agonizing snail-pace prattle in the vaulted palaces of the diplomats. Our leaders are not all unbalanced madmen like Captain Ahab, who in their hate-filled search for the white whale would sink their own ship and drown their own crew. No, they are, on the whole, sane, dedicated, hard-working men who are trying desperately to achieve the best of both possible worlds.

The trick is to strike a balance by preserving the old prerogatives and privileges and profiteering and positions and protocol while at the same time juggling the deadly thermonuclear bombs. In the cynical tradition of Talleyrand, our leaders have coined a new term to describe this delicate balancing act: deterrence.

What does this deterrence, about which we hear so much, actually mean? It is an unwritten, three-corner mutual suicide pact between NATO, the Warsaw powers, and Red China which reflects the present temporary stalemate of weapons capable of mutual annihilation; and the guardians of this pact are the nuclear weapons themselves. Yet, strangely enough, despite the highly advanced technology, deterrence resembles more and more the stylized jousts of the feudal period, which were as much a test of will as a trial of strength. It is a game of Russian roulette —with the life of civilization at stake—where the credibility of each contestant is measured by his show of iron nerve, his reckless resolve, his noisy bluster, his intransigent truculence, his self-proclaimed toughness of fiber— in short, a game of psychological bluff.

The best description of the operation of the theory of deterrence is given by Bertrand Russell. He calls it the game of chicken. It works like this: suppose there are two opposing gangs of hotrodders contesting for possession of a dragstrip. Each gang piles into its jalopy and heads full speed ahead on a collision course toward the enemy vehicle. The trick of the sport is that the right wheels of one and the left wheels of the other car must ride on the center line. The first gang that loses its nerve and swerves is chicken and loses. To show their determination, the drivers throw away their steering wheels, drive blindfold and guzzle whiskey. This sport has also been called nuclear neurosis.

Deterrence thus confronts a nation with the choice between brinkmanship and surrender. And mankind has advanced to the brink and peered over into the eternal abyss on more than one occasion in recent times. How long can man teeter on the edge and not fall over in this age of continuous tension and trigger-happy belligerency? How many times will he be able to step back?

Thus, when our leaders tell us that this nation "has the fortitude to risk war" and "we are prepared," they are talking sheer, meaningless nonsense. They must know that there can be only one result in a modern war—automatic mutual suicide. Our military and political leaders persist in bravely talking about a "win policy" when they

know, or should know, that victory in war—or even defense—is no longer possible: only retaliation is. They do
not tell us that retaliation will come only after most of
us, and of them, are dead. They do not tell us that if
deterrence fails then both deterrer and deterred alike are
destroyed.

The great danger is that with so many atomic missiles
stockpiled like cordwood, with so many buttons that might
be pushed by so many fingers, with so much scientific
progress creating ever more automatic doomsday machines allowing less and less scope for human intervention;
military technology will take over and decide our fate.
Mankind has been unbelievably lucky so far. One serious
miscalculation, one accident, one irrational act, one error
of judgment, one case of mechanical or human failure, one
psychotic or berserk individual, one act of sabotage, one
lost nerve or head, one madman, one false alarm, and the
civilization of centuries goes up in smoke.

Read human history: it is a chronicle of human folly
that reeks with blunders and mistakes and lusts and cu-
pidities and inanities and madness. It is the fiasco of the
Bag of Pigs repeated over and over again to the point of
nausea. We need only examine our own lives and experi-
ences to realize how frail man is and how nothing ever
goes according to plan or is foolproof. Common sense tells
us that we have no right to count on man's ability to avoid
fatal mistakes permanently. If we have learned anything
for certain in this world, it is that accidents will happen.

Our leaders, including the President himself, have gone
to great pains to reassure us that every precaution has
been taken to prevent any mechanical or emotional malfunction. Articles like that of one-time Deputy Secretary

of Defense Roswell L. Gilpatric in the *New York Times Magazine* of May 17, 1964, entitled "Strangelove? Seven Days? Not Likely" and books like the *Fail Safe Fallacy* by Sidney Hook detail the "wide array of administrative and physical restraints on a nuclear firing in violation of authority." It is stressed that this authority is the special responsibility of the President of the United States and that he alone has ultimate personal control over the use of nuclear weapons. A conscientious attempt has been made to extend the doctrine of papal infallibility to the office of the Presidency.

Now, suppose that the present incumbent in the White House is a prudent, not impulsive, man whom we hold in the highest regard and respect. Suppose that there is no doubt he can be trusted with this awesome and fearful responsibility. Granted, it is a little difficult for one who has been nurtured in our democratic way of life to reconcile himself to this devolution of infinite power upon one man even if he happens to be the President of the United States. Apparently, the form of government has turned full cycle and has reverted to the ancient absolutism, except that no oriental potentate, not even Xerxes or Justinian or Kublai Khan, ever had the power to decide the life or death, not only of individuals, but of the entire world.

What troubles this writer is the thought that perhaps it is only a pretense that the Chief Executive will be in a position to make that awful, lonely, and terrible decision—even if his code-carrying military officer were at hand. Decisions, after all, can be based only on information received. With the development of weaponry having so inhumanely compressed the time available to make the most fearful decisions, it is highly problematical that even the most advanced electronic communication network could provide the required data in time. When the chips are down, decisions will nevertheless be made in the only place where they can be made—in the theatre of operations. As a matter of fact, articles in *Time* and *U.S. News and World Report* magazines have stated that such prior authority has already been delegated to the NATO, North American Air Defense and other commands. The authority to NATO commanders dates back to 1954 when they were empowered to use tactical nuclear weapons in case of need to stop the "Soviet hordes."

Suppose one could, despite his misgivings, learn to sleep confidently with the fact that his life and the lives of his loved ones rested in the hands of the President of the United States. One could never be comfortable with the awareness that this same power over life and death lies simultaneously with the leaders of Britain, China, France, and the Soviet Union. This anxiety is further aggravated by the instability inherent in the anarchic process of succession in the Soviet Union, Red China and elsewhere.

Continued life under deterrence is absolutely dependent upon the rationality of the world's leaders. How can one possibly trust so many diverse personalities? Suppose a future President of the United States is more impulsive and tends to shoot from the hip. Suppose, as has happened too many times before, a madman or a soldier of fortune or an idiot or a fool ascends to power in any one of a half a dozen countries.

In short, our leaders do not dare to come forth and admit that their policies are bankrupt, that they can no longer provide us with the protection and security which is their reason for being. All they can do is to meet threat with counter-threat, blackmail with counter-blackmail. They have no plan or program to deal with the failure of deterrence or accidental war except to make the prospect so dreadful that it is hoped that everyone will be careful in advance. The harsh fact is that the military and political leaders who are supposed to be the guardians of our safety are actually the greatest threat to our continued existence.

So much for our leaders who are herding us toward Armageddon. Now what about the people—the people, yes, the humble citizens—what are they doing in this "most dangerous time in the history of the human race" "when the last ding-dong of doom" is clanging. Are they raging and howling against their fate? Our very skins are at stake; how are we showing that we care like hell?

Suppose there were an epidemic; we certainly would be demanding, in no uncertain terms, that immediate steps be taken to safeguard our health. For instance, a typhoid epidemic broke out in Aberdeen, Scotland, during June, 1964; at least 450 persons were stricken with the disease. As a result of public outcry, the local authorities closed the ancient public toilets—which had no washing facilities —opened new ones, and gave the city its most thorough scrubbing since medieval times. At least two new public health and sanitation organizations were formed. The most universal of all human instincts, that of survival, was threatened and the people reacted.

The greatest scourge in man's history—the threat of atomic war and universal death—stalks the world. The atomic physicist Ralph E. Lapp best describes our reaction: "The strangest aspect of our perilous time is the ominous quiet. Probably never in history has the human race looked so much like sheep marching silently to slaughter." We are like the shepherds who placidly continue to tend their flocks on the slopes of Mt. Vesuvius while the volcano rumbles and trembles underneath their feet. One stands aghast, appalled, irritated, and infuriated by this heedless unconcern—this curious, sinister atmosphere of somnambulism. The danger is frightening enough. What is even more frightening is that the danger is so little appreciated.

At the same time, what is the popular attitude towards disarmament? Let Jerome B. Wiesner, the first Presidential special assistant for science and technology express it: "That word disarmament—it's pretty suspect. It has come to mean softness, unpreparedness, appeasement. Everybody says he's for disarmament, but discuss it as a serious hope and you're likely to be patronized as unrealistic. It's hard to believe, but self-preservation has become a controversial issue."

Yet, this writer refuses to accept the proposition that mankind has forfeited the race, has thrown in the towel, and embraced the bomb. It cannot be that we have completely defaulted on our obligations to our children. We must continue to assume that man wants to live, not to die. Man's holiest and dearest possession is life; there is no wealth but life. Life, even the hardest, is the most beautiful, wonderful, and most miraculous treasure on earth. The continuation of life must stand above all causes and all differences.

Pope John XXIII could not have been mistaken when he urged the heads of states to "give ear to the anguished cry of peace! peace! which rises up to Heaven from every part of the world, from innocent children and those grown old, from individuals and communities." The Russian children cannot be mistaken in their yearning for this blessing which is "greater than any other" when they sing their popular song:

> Let there always be skies,
> Let there always be mama,
> Let there always be me.

Surely there must exist in this world a sufficient number of men of good will, with a common interest in the continuation of life and civilization, who will band together to save the future for our children, to ensure that there will still be an earth upon which our children might walk. There is still time to recapture control of our destinies and to reassert the fundamental sovereignty of the individual upon which all government rests. War need not be accepted by man in the same spirit of resignation in which he must accept a natural calamity like an earthquake, a volcanic eruption or a tidal wave. War is manmade and it is within the power of man to abolish it.

The citizen is irrevocably involved in the issues of war and peace because upon their resolution depends his very life, the lives of his children and of his children's children for ever and ever and ever. The words of the prophecy have come to pass: "I call heaven and earth to record this day against you, that I have set before you life and death, blessing and cursing. Will you therefore choose life that both thou and thy seed may live?"

Many readers will recall the scene in Bertolt Brecht's *Mother Courage and Her Children* where the mute Kattrin pounds the drums to alert the sleeping town to the

invading army. This is precisely the purpose of this book
—to alert the sleeping citizen to the danger, to ignite the
public indignation, to bestir our conscience. This book is
offered in the firm conviction that George Washington
spoke truthfully when he said, "The mass of citizens in
these United States will always act well whenever they
can obtain a right understanding of matters."

Now, many other books have been written on disarmament—this most vital of all subjects—and many of these
works have been written by learned professors and scholars. This writer urges you to read as many of these books
as possible but he defies you to come away from such
reading with the slightest inkling of what this most serious subject of disarmament is all about. Unfortunately,
this entire field of study has been so thoroughly wrapped
in the mythology of the times and so utterly corrupted
by the lure of research and development contracts, that
it has become almost impossible to winnow the fact from
the fiction.

Thus, where understanding is so obscured and the peril
so real and imminent and tangible and terrible, no alarm
can be too hysterical or too shrill or repeated often enough.

In order for man to survive this age so that we do not
go down in history—if there will be a history—as the guilty
generation which did nothing to prevent the annihilation
of mankind itself, a way out must be found. The solution
will certainly not be a simple one. The road to peace is
a long and arduous one, beset by mountain ranges of
difficulties and complications and setbacks. It will not be
achieved until the feeling for peace is woven into the
fabric of human behavior and the values of peace have
penetrated into the minds of men. One thing is certain:

either men will learn to live together as brothers or they
will die together as fools.

Perhaps the answer will be found to lie in a world state
or a loose confederation of sovereign states or a series
of supranational authorities organized on a functional
basis or a system of international law or some other arrangement. Or perhaps we will finally determine with
General von Möltke that eternal peace is only a dream
and not a beautiful dream at that. In any event, the important consideration is that mankind desperately needs time
in order to think and grope its way out of its present
perilous dilemma. We must somehow recapture the time
that has been erased by the atomic bomb.

Too much time has already been lost. What is still possible today may be impossible tomorrow. Yesterday, the
United States alone had the bomb. Then it was the turn
of Britain and Russia and France. Today Red China is
heard from. Tomorrow? Every day and every hour counts
in this eleventh hour of man's race toward self-destruc-
tion. In the old days the problem was the simple one of
war or peace: today the issue is oblivion or peace. We
seem to think that we can go on indefinitely without making up our minds concerning these two alternatives of
the atomic age. Perhaps we can; but the risks are enormous, and in flirting with atomic war we play with oblivion. As Jane Addams stated so eloquently on the occasion
of her designation as Nobel laureate in 1935, "Nothing
could be worse than the fear that one had given up too
soon and had left one effort unexpended which might
have saved the world." President Kennedy summed up,
"Each day we draw nearer the hour of maximum danger."

Are we condemned, like Moses, to perish within sight

of the promised land? Civilization can gain the required time to mature to the stage of its technology only if it draws the fangs of the atomic monster which bestrides its path. This can be accomplished only by *disarmament*, something which the United Nations General Assembly, on November 2, 1959, unanimously termed "the most important question facing the world today." Here, according to Secretary General U Thant of the United Nations, is our greatest challenge; and according to President Johnson, "the most important task on earth and the ultimate test of our century." Chairman Khrushchev concurred, "There is one problem whose solution is awaited with hope by the peoples of all countries, big and small, irrespective of their social system and way of life. This is the problem of disarmament." The Camp David communiqué agreed that the question of disarmament is the most important one facing the world today.

Certainly, armaments are only a symptom of international tension and not their cause. But disarmament negotiation cannot await the settlement of international political problems. Such a course of inaction would be too dangerous. The argument that armaments per se do not lead to war is very much like saying that alcohol does not lead to drunkenness. In a sense, that is true. But without alcohol there would be no drunkenness and without armaments there would be no war. The mere existence of the armaments is an invitation to their use. Was the Nagasaki bomb used simply because it was there?

Of course, disarmament is only the beginning, not the completion of the solution of the problem of war and peace. But the easing of the arms race would surely create an international atmosphere that would be more conducive to the resolution of world differences. Disarmament today is not one question among many others; it is the one vital question: to be or not to be. Its shadow falls on our every action, step, thought, or dream. Tomorrow will not dawn unless this question is resolved. The choice is between demilitarization and destruction of our civilization.

The hopes and expectations of all humanity, which had been kindled by the signing of the test ban treaty on August 5, 1963, have all but evaporated. The ratification of this treaty by 107 nations has not been the forerunner of meaningful disarmament negotiation. Instead, the arms race rushes forward with undiminished intensity. The "shaft of light cut into the darkness" has been blotted out.

Alerted by Dr. Linus Carl Pauling and others to the danger of radioactive fallout to present and future generations, an almost hysterical concern swept around the world. A great outcry arose against the reckless testing that was befouling the planetary environment and threatening to make the earth uninhabitable. Perhaps the test ban treaty was only a sop thrown to dampen public hysteria. Nevertheless, the halt to the contamination of the air we breathe and the food we eat is no small boon and mankind is grateful.

The point to be made here is that the issue of atomic testing was approached from its least important aspect—the biological damage that was being done. The test ban conferences were health conferences—not disarmament conferences. Of course, it is much easier to arouse public concern over matters concerning public health. But in this process of simplification, the demonstrators and the agitators overlooked other reasons for outlawing atmospheric testing, which far outweigh the biological arguments in their impact upon the future of mankind. These over-looked reasons are the arms race and the technological race to perfect ever more deadly means of annihilation. The technological race continues unabated and the atomic tests continue underground. There is still a need for the Aldermaston marchers, the pickets, the sit-downers, the hunger strikers. Much work remains to be done before mankind will hear the final command, "Ground Arms."

Yes, this is a time for hysteria.

2

The Subject Matter

What is the cause of the hysteria which grips the world? Let us take a few moments to picture the current state of man: that of an arms economy and a weapon culture staggering under a mountain of armaments which is wholly unrelated to any sane or feasible military objective.

Over 20,000,000 men are under arms in the services of the various nations of the world. Over $130 billion a year is being spent by the powers for military purposes. (Add to this sum the lost produce of the lost labor of 20 million of our healthiest, most vigorous, youngest men.) This arms budget is a sum in excess of the entire income of the two-thirds of the peoples of the world who must live in the most abject poverty, unable to satisfy the primal needs of animal life. All the great powers are now spending about twice as great a proportion of their national income on armaments as they did in the interwar years.

The United States Defense Department alone is spending $79.8 billion a year for military purposes. This budget maintains a force of 3,477,000 military personnel and 1,093,000 civilians. This force is supported by an arsenal that boasts a complete spectrum of weapons, ranging down from the twenty-five megaton thermonuclear bomb to noxious gases. This array is designed to cope with general atomic war, limited atomic war, conventional war, and guerilla insurgency. This profusion is called "The Mix." The Defense Department thus constitutes, by far, the largest enterprise of the capitalistic, free enterprise United States, with a budget of $80 billion and property holdings valued at $183.6 billion.

Now, the popular conception of an atom bomb is that of a city-buster with the force of at least twenty megatons, roughly the equivalent of a solid block of TNT piled as high as the Empire State Building and covering six city blocks. It is not generally known that atomic weapons now come in the widest possible variety of sizes, ranging down to a cute little nuclear artillery shell only six inches in diameter carrying a warhead with a sub-kiloton explosive force.

This little gadget will be fired by the 155-mm. howitzer, a standard battlefield support piece with a range of up to ten miles. Except for the 105-mm. howitzer, most of the principal artillery pieces, including the 155-mm. howitzer, the eight-inch howitzer, the 175-mm. self-propelled gun and the 280-mm. cannon can now boast of nuclear warheads. These comparatively smaller-yield rockets and missiles carrying atomic warheads are called nuclear tactical weapons and bear fetching names like the Davy Crockett (a bazooka-like weapon which can be mounted on a jeep or carried by troops but which is to be replaced by a more accurate and efficient weapon),

Sergeant, Honest John, Little John, Corporal, Lacrosse, Pershing, Shellelagh, Lance, etc. Even tanks like the General Sheridan have been equipped with atomic firepower.

There are even reports of a gun-tube type of tactical nuclear weapon with a force of one kiloton that is so destructive against massed tank or ground troop advances that it had to be withdrawn over the protests of high ranking military officers.

Tactical and larger nuclear weapons are deployed with front line American and allied troops although the atomic ammunition is supposedly stored separately. However, it has been revealed that the ostensible American control existed more in principle than in fact. For over six years, the United States Defense Department concealed custody arrangements under which the fighter bombers and missiles of nine NATO allies, including West Germany, were armed with American atomic warheads. And how are these nuclear armed planes guarded? The answer is by no less than two American armed sentries. This protection must be as effective as the formidable guard over the balance of the nuclear stockpile, consisting of nothing less than police dogs, sentries and searchlights. Where are the burglar-proof locks? The answer, of course, is that there are virtually no restraints except the honor of the ally.

The Russians have similarly positioned their tactical and other nuclear weapons among the Warsaw powers. Only God knows if they have been any more careful with their nuclear ammunition.

To illustrate the magnitude of this situation, it is interesting to note that Secretary McNamara reported to NATO, on June 2, 1965, that Western nuclear strength in Europe had been increased by 10 per cent in the first five months of 1965 and 100 per cent since 1961, and that the stockpile numbered in the thousands. The present estimate is over 7,000.

This arming was carried out despite the misgivings which had been expressed earlier by the Secretary to the Armed Services Committee of the House of Representatives, on January 30, 1963: "Nuclear weapons, even in the lower kiloton ranges, are extremely destructive devices and hardly the preferred weapons to defend such heavily populated areas as Europe. Furthermore, while it does not necessarily follow that the use of tactical nuclear weapons must inevitably escalate into global nuclear war, it does present a very definite threshold, beyond which we enter a vast unknown."

Since the average nuclear tactical weapon has a yield five times that of the bomb dropped on Hiroshima (twenty kilotons) and "can blow up a hell of a lot of territory," the firebreak line between nuclear and conventional arms is being obliterated. In effect, these comparatively low-yield tactical nuclear weapons represent a form of internal proliferation. The military is increasingly regarding nuclear weapons as simply high explosives writ large. They have not seemed to grasp that their destructive power makes them a completely new kind of military force. The atom bomb is increasingly being regarded as merely another field weapon.

In this connection, a report, submitted to the United Nations on October 24, 1967, by an international panel of nuclear experts, found that if 400 small nuclear weapons (not an unreasonably large number) were used in a European battle area, "the physical damage caused would correspond to something like six times that caused by all the bombing of World War II—and all sustained in a few days rather than a few years. It is clear enough that the destruction and disruption which would result from so-called tactical nuclear warfare would hardly differ from the effects of strategic war in the area concerned."

To deliver the larger size nuclear bombs, with an explosive force upwards of half a megaton, the United States has built no less than three separate delivery systems—for land, air, and sea. In order to comprehend the significance of the figures cited below, it should be kept in mind that one missile or bomber can deliver more explosive force than was released by both sides in all of World War II.

The United States goal is 1,054 intercontinental ballistic missiles. This land system is comprised of 54 Titan II's, and the balance Minuteman I's, II's, and III's.

The Minuteman I missile is a first-generation solid fuel weapon capable of hurling a nuclear warhead with the explosive equivalent of one million tons of TNT at targets 6,300 miles away. The Minuteman II is an improved model with a range of more than 9,000 miles with twice the accuracy and 30 per cent more of a warhead. A new improved Minuteman III, designed to carry multiple independently targetable warheads and penetration devices is being substituted for the 650 older, smaller Minuteman I's.

These nuclear missiles are based underground in individually dispersed blast-resistant concrete and steel silos. In contrast to the discontinued liquid-fueled Atlas, both the Titan and the Minuteman are known as instant ICBM's that are propelled by solid fuels which are stored within the weapons and which can be fired in less than one minute.

The powerful 108-foot long, 330,000-pound Titan II can carry a nuclear payload equal to eighteen megatons over 6,000 miles at a speed of over 15,000 miles per hour.

Although the strategic forces of the future will place principal reliance upon ballistic missiles, as the preferred "primary weapon for the assured destruction mission," the strategic bomber force is very much in the picture. The United States Strategic Air Command (SAC) can put into the air 697 manned intercontinental B-52, B-58 and FB-111 heavy bombers. Each of these bombers is equipped with decoy missiles and other penetration aids to assure that they will reach their targets. There are 540 strategic or long range bombers constantly on a fifteen-minute alert.

Present plans call for scrapping all eighty of the B-58's and all but 250 of the G and H models of the B-52 by 1971; 210 new FB-111's will be introduced as the older planes are phased out. Since the American heavy bomber force was four times as large as that of the Soviet Union when these plans were announced, it was the opinion of Secretary McNamara that the United States would continue to have a comparable advantage even after the changeover.

It is still doubtful whether Congress will acquiesce in this program. The manned bomber lobby is very powerful. In 1961, Congress appropriated $525 million for B-52 and B-58 armed bombers that the Defense Department didn't want. In 1966, Congress appropriated nearly $12 million more than the Administration had requested for preliminary work associated with a new strategic bomber.

The nuclear striking arm of the United States Navy consists of 107 nuclear submarines, including 41 armed with 16 intermediate-range Polaris A-3 missiles each. These missiles can be fired from under water and carry a thermonuclear warhead with an explosive power of about 800 kilotons. The Navy is spending $2 billion to develop and produce a new Poseidon missile to replace the A-3 on thirty-one of the submarines. Although the range of 2,800 miles will remain the same, the new multiple warhead missile will have about twice the explosive power and double the accuracy of the old projectile.

Back in March, 1962, when the Navy had only 14 Polaris submarines equipped with the more primitive A-1 and A-2, Secretary Paul H. Nitze stated that the power and reliability of the Polaris fleet alone was such that it could eliminate most of the warmaking capabilities of the Soviet urban industrial complex and kill 25 to 35 million people. And the nuclear submarine is well-nigh invulnerable. Instead of the old problem of countries without navies, we may well end up with navies without countries.

All in all, the United States nuclear arsenal must have close to 100,000 nuclear weapons in its stockpile with a firepower which Dr. Linus C. Pauling estimates to be equivalent to 240,000 megatons. What does a megaton mean? Translated into human terms, how many acres of skin sloughed off how many people does it represent? How many bushels of fallen-out hair does it measure? How many baskets of eyes melted into fluid running down how many cheeks? How many yards of festering sores? How many liters of blood?

In the opinion of Professor Pauling, the total American megatonage is sufficient to destroy the Soviet Union twelve times over. Elsewhere, Professor Seymour Melman estimated that the United States has the overkill capability to destroy 140 major Soviet cities anywhere from 78 to 1,250 times, depending on assumptions. Such is the awful arithmetic of the United States atomic arsenal.

But the propensity toward human error being what it is, one can never be deadly sure that every single enemy individual could be satisfactorily obliterated by the American nuclear stockpile. A few might, God forbid, survive the holocaust. So, to make absolutely certain, the United States has duplicated its nuclear destructive power with a full panoply of conventional arms.

In the main, conventional armaments comprise the old-fashioned, garden-variety weapons of the good old days: bullets, grenades, bayonets, rifles, flame throwers, machine guns, mortars, artillery, bazookas, jeeps, tanks. A few new gadgets have been added in the proving ground of Vietnam, such as the bizarre piggy-back bullet, the terrifying cluster bomb unit (C.B.U.) and the Lazy Dog bomb carrying 10,000 slivers of razor-sharp steel flechettes. The United States Air Force still boasts 138 squadrons with thousands of fighter attack planes equipped with rockets, napalm, block busters and a new exotic snakeye bomb. In addition to its nuclear powered Polaris-carrying submarines, the United States Navy can still launch no less than 3,400 vessels ranging from the landing barge to the mighty aircraft carrier.

Whatever tenuous line is still maintained between the nuclear and the conventional weapon is based on the distinction that nuclear weapons, even the smallest, kill primarily by radiation and not by blast.

Despite the comfort of this overwhelming nuclear and conventional power, a gnawing doubt persists. Suppose, in spite of everything, an enemy or allied individual—or an American—might perchance survive. This cannot possibly be. Perhaps it is not enough to merely rip, tear, burn or mutilate the body. The body must also be poisoned.

To accomplish this most worthwhile and desired objective, scientists at the University of Pennsylvania are experimenting on how to poison a nation's rice supply and this chemical has actually been sprayed from the air in South Vietnam, blighting hundreds of thousands of acres.

The United States Army chemical-biological warfare service maintains installations at Fort Detrick and Edgewood Arsenal, Maryland, Dugway Proving Ground, Utah, Pine Bluff, Arkansas, the Rocky Mountain Arsenal, and the Newport Chemical Plant, Indiana, for breeding and increasing manifold the virulence of the pathogenic organisms that produce every deadly and loathesome disease known to medical science, including plant as well as human pestilence. Carried by airborne particles of solid or liquid organisms called aerosols in biological clouds, infectious diseases like anthrax, botulism, tularemia, yellow fever, cholera, plague and influenza can easily be spread around the world in minimum time.

The chemical-biological warfare service has also succeeded in developing a wide variety of asphyxiating or deleterious gases, including the well-known will-destroying nerve gases and derivatives of lysergic acid which cause temporary or permanent insanity. Nerve gas tests killed 6,400 sheep in Utah's Skull Valley during March, 1968. There are also odorless pacifying gases which cause instant diarrhea.

Since CB weapons, like nuclear arms, form a continuous spectrum from the temporarily incapacitating to the highly lethal, the same dangers are involved. Once the restraints are breached, who can tell where the escalation will end?

The Congress appropriates more than $158,000,000 per year for this grisly business. But perhaps Dr. Paul Weiss of the Rockefeller Institute, a member of the President's Scientific Advisory Committee, had the more proper approach when he wrote in the *Nation* of April 30, 1960: "We must convince the scientific community that chemical and biological warfare is not a dirty business. It is no worse than other means of killing." Frank J. Granzeier writes in the magazine *Industrial Research*, "It would be sheer madness for any country, knowing its potential enemies have stockpiled toxic weapons, not to follow suit." One wonders whether it ever occeurred to Mr. Granzeier that toxic chemical and biological weapons might, in themselves, be sheer madness.

These experts do not mention the forbidden island of Gruinard, off the remote northwest coast of Scotland. British germ warfare experiments there during World War II have contaminated the island for 100 years. One cannot help remarking at the full circle that has been turned by science: from finding cures for disease back to creating germs to create plagues. In fact, researchers have created, among others, a strain of Pasteurella pestis (plague bacteria) which is even resistant to antibiotics. Such research calls to mind the experiments of the mad Nazi scientists.

One might expect that the American people, having created this overwhelming juggernaut of destruction, would be content with its handiwork and relax from its labors. Heaven forbid! Never! On the contrary, the American people are working ever more feverishly to devise and build increasingly more monstrous and fiendish implements of death. This arms race gone berserk can have only one end: the ultimate weapon, in the shape of a neutron or cobalt or asteroid bomb, and universal and total death to all life—human, animal and plant.

Almost $7 billion a year is being spent by the United States government for weapons research and development. Secretary of Defense Robert S. McNamara told the Democratic Platform Committee, on August 17, 1964, that the Kennedy-Johnson administration had increased by 50 per cent the expenditures for military research and development over the level prevailing during the last four years of the previous Eisenhower administration, and had initiated 208 weapons research projects with 77 costing $10 million or more each.

In addition, the space budget of over $7 billion annually is basically military motivated. Any doubt on this score was removed by President Johnson's order to the Air Force, announced in the wake of the historic flight of Gemini 5 in August, 1965, to develop a $1.5 billion secret military manned orbiting laboratory (M.O.L.). By underlining the essential military significance of space, the President has doomed any prospects of a cooperative effort by the United States and the Soviet Union to put a man on the moon. Such a project had been advanced by the Vatican.

President Johnson told educators in Nashville, Tennessee, on March 15, 1967, that satellite reconnaissance alone had justified spending ten times the $35 to $40 billion that the nation had spent on space. Because of this reconnaissance, "I know how many missiles the enemy has," he said. The Air Force admitted, in April, 1967, that photos from weather satellites were used to aid the bombing runs over Vietnam.

Dr. John S. Foster, Jr., Director of Defense Research and Engineering, announced in a speech in Dallas on December 13, 1967, that the United States was developing a "space bus," or MIRV (for Multiple Independently Targeted Re-entry Vehicle) that can drop off hydrogen bombs, city by city, over enemy territory. Two such MIRV's were successfully tested on August 16, 1968. And in early September, 1968 came word that the Soviet Union had also tested a multiple warhead rocket.

Despite the treaty for peaceful uses of outer space, the world faces the terrifying prospect of an arms race in space.

At a military parade in Moscow on November 7, 1965, the Soviets displayed a 115-foot-long three-stage rocket that Tass described as an orbital missile. The official press agency went on to state that the warheads of the weapon "can deliver their surprise blow on the first or any other orbit around the earth." Beginning with a flight, on September 17, 1966, from Tyuratam in Kazakhstan, the Soviets have been testing the firing of nuclear bombs from space, with only three minutes' warning, through Fractional Orbital Bombardment (FOBS) and Multiple Orbit Bombardment (MOBS) systems. In November, 1967, Colonel General Vladimir F. Tolubko, first deputy commander of the Strategic Rocket Troops, even dropped the Russian fiction of innocence concerning the military value of space, and boasted that "soldiers-rocket men" had launched almost everything sent into space by the Soviet Union in the last decade.

In his 1963 economic report to the Congress, President Kennedy had stated that "The defense, space and atomic energy activities of the country absorb about two-thirds of the trained people available for exploring our scientific

and technical frontiers." In 1961, of 400,000 scientists and
engineers in the United States doing research and development work, 250,000 were doing it for space and defense. Since 1954, the number of research and development scientists and engineers in industry has increased
by 160,000, but all but 30,000 of these have been absorbed
by projects for the government. War is the new mother
of invention.

Thus, while only 33⅓ per cent of American research
is devoted to non-military purposes, countries like Germany and Japan are applying up to 85 per cent of their
research effort to automate, modernize and equip industrial plants. Perhaps the fact that such a large proportion
of American inventive genius is being buried in underground silos to await Doomsday explains the relatively
high unemployment rate in the United States and the
failure of this country to grow productively at the same
rate as other highly industrialized nations. Such is the
double price that the arms race is imposing on the American people.

The private sector of the economy will have to be
satisfied with the crumbs which may fall from the draw-
ing tables of science and technology. One is inevitably
reminded of Jonathan Swift's Academy of Legado, where
the people are so proud of their great center of useless
invention while at the same time "the whole country lies
in waste, the houses are in ruins and the people are without food and clothes." That is why Professor Seymour
Melman terms the United States a "depleted society,"
operating the oldest stock of metal working machinery
of any industrial country in the world.

With only 20 cents out of the government's dollar going

to sustain its civilization and all the rest going for instruments of torture and death; with 10.6 per cent of the total national income being allocated for war and preparation for war; with its military personnel and arms being deployed in more than 300 bases, facilities, posts and stations in 30 countries overseas; with one-quarter to one-third of the economic activity of the nation based on the weapons race; with over eight million persons earning their living from defense spending; the United States must be classified as a warfare state.

But as President Johnson has so truly said, "The guns and the bombs, the rockets and the warships, are all symbols of human failure." Today the armed strength of the United States is stronger than the combined might of all the nations in the entire history of the world—stronger than any adversary or combination of adversaries. President Johnson has described this force as such that compared to it "the combined destructive power of every battle ever fought by man is like a firecracker thrown against the sun." At the same time, President Johnson pledged "that the United States is, and will remain, first in the use of science and technology for the protection of its people."

Thus, as we stand in proper awe before the most formidable military establishment the world has ever known with "an aggregation of force without parallel in human history," we must not forget the other side of the coin. And that is that we are, at the same time, contemplating in the United States a nation that is the most abject failure in all human recorded history. Nor is this failure only a rhetorical figure of speech. It is an actual, real, terrifying failure. We are faced with the realization that the weapons available to us are fantastically destructive while the means at our disposal for preventing destruction from such weapons are woefully inadequate.

President Johnson has "repeatedly stated his conviction that steadily mounting nuclear stock does not insure the security of any nation." Former Secretary of Defense Robert S. McNamara himself postulated what he called "an essential fact"—"that the sheer multiplication of a nation's destructive nuclear capability does not necessarily produce a net increase in its security." So, as we pour more and more resources and money and skill into increasing armaments, we are, on balance, enjoying less and less security. We have what statisticians call a "dose-rate" curve—the more, the worse.

In 1946, neither the Soviet Union nor any other possible adversary was in a position to endanger the shores of continental United States. At most, the Soviets might have been able to launch an attack across the Bering Strait through Alaska. In such an attack the United States might conceivably have suffered casualties of one, or perhaps two, million persons after a long-drawn-out, bloody struggle.

Twenty years and $850 billion later, of which $28 billion was spent for atomic bombs, it is possible for the American people to suffer casualties estimated at 100 million persons in a single day should the Russians unleash an attack. Nor have we devised any defense to minimize these casualties. It is possible that shelters might to some extent mitigate the devastating toll but the American people, in their wisdom, have evidently come to the conclusion that there will be no escape on Judgment Day and that any survivors would envy the dead.

At this point, it is timely to hear the testimony upon this subject from the world's outstanding expert, Robert S. McNamara. He told the House Committee on Armed Services during 1963 Hearings on the Military Posture: "It will become increasingly difficult, regardless of the form of the attack, to destroy a sufficiently large proportion of the Soviet's strategic nuclear forces to preclude major damage to the United States regardless of how large or what kind of strategic forces we build.

"Even if we were to double and triple our forces we would not be able to destroy quickly all or almost all of the hardened ICBM sites. And even if we could do that, we know no way to destroy the enemy's missile launching submarines at the same time. We do not anticipate that either the United States or the Soviet Union will acquire that capability in the foreseeable future.

"Moreover, to minimize damage to the United States, such a force would also have to be accompanied by an extensive missile defense system and a much more elaborate civil defense system than has, thus far, been contemplated.

"Even then, we could not preclude casualties counted in the tens of millions."

In January, 1966, Secretary McNamara told the same congressional committee that under the most favorable— but unlikely—conditions, where the United States unleashed the initial nuclear strike, the *least* number of American fatalities from inevitable retaliation would be 25 million.

To round out this brief sketch of the might of the free world, we must add to the forces of the arsenal of the western world another 2.5 million men under arms in the other NATO nations, together with their conventional armaments and the widow's mite of atomic power held by France and Britain. Britain is spending about $6 billion a year of its limited funds on defense while France's megalomania is costing her almost an equivalent amount. The remaining NATO powers are allotting about $3 billion annually for military purposes.

American satellites like South Vietnam, South Korea and Taiwan contribute an additional two million soldiers together with their arms. The nations of the British Commonwealth and of the French community of nations complete the roster of armed strength presently mobilized by the West—a truly staggering aggregation of might.

Thomas Hobbes wrote in the seventeenth century, "in all times, Kings, Persons of Sovereign authority, because of their independency, are in continual jealousies and in the state and posture of gladiators; having their weapons pointing and their eyes fixed on one another, that is, their forts, garrisons and guns upon the frontiers of their kingdoms and continual spies upon their neighbors; which is a posture of war."

This description certainly holds true today. We have described above the posture of war maintained today by the free world. Let us crawl under the barbed wire of the iron curtain in an attempt to describe another armed camp—that of the Warsaw powers and its principal protagonist, the Union of Soviet Socialist Republics. Since the Soviet Union is a closed society, information concerning its posture of war is not so readily available. But enough is known to permit us to draw a reasonably accurate picture.

The total Soviet military budget is estimated at $33

billion annually by the London Institute of Strategic Studies—roughly 17 per cent of the gross national product. The Institute estimated the Soviet manpower in active service at 3,220,000 plus 250,000 security and border troops.

Dr. Linus C. Pauling calculated the Soviet nuclear arsenal at 80,000 megatons, sufficient to wipe out the United States eight times over. Professor Edward Teller has stated that there is a considerable probability that Soviet nuclear explosives are superior to those of the United States, with a real city-buster that is rated at 100 megatons.

It is believed that half of the Soviet's ICBM's boast warheads of thirty megatons or more. Two of these bombs should be sufficient to destroy New York City and its suburbs and engulf New England and the middle Atlantic states in radioactive fire. It should be kept in mind that the explosive power of a single thermonuclear bomb is greater than the total explosive power of all ammunition used in all the wars of the past including the first two world wars of this century. The Soviets have already tested two tremendous bombs, one of thirty and one of fifty-eight megatons. The Soviet atomic stockpile must also be counted in the tens of thousands of weapons, with a wide range of tactical atomic warheads.

To deliver these warheads, the Russians are now producing mobile and hardened-based, solid-fueled SS-9 and SS-11 intercontinental ballistic missiles, roughly comparable to the Minutemen and Polaris. The Soviet Union is reputed to be approaching parity with the United States and to have close to 1,000 operational ICBM's and 700 to 800 MRBM's and IRBM's. Back in 1961, Chairman

Khrushchev boasted that Russia had a rocket that could "hit a fly in outer space." The Russian strategic air force boasts about 200 Bison and Bear heavy bombers and about 1,000 Badger and Blinder medium bombers.

According to the authoritative *Jane's Fighting Ships*, the Soviet Union is rapidly building a formidable Navy with 55 operational nuclear powered submarines that can launch 150 Polaris-type Serb missiles from an underwater position. In addition, approximately forty-five older conventional diesel-powered submarines have been converted and fitted with missiles, including some with limited underwater firing capability. All in all, the Soviet submarine fleet numbers 425, unmatched by any other power.

The Russian surface fleet, the second largest, is composed of over 2,200 vessels, ranging in size from cruisers to landing craft. The first aircraft carrier is being built. Further, because of the nature of the Soviet system, the entire merchant shipping fleet of 9 million deadweight tons, is regarded "as a vital fourth arm of defense in emergencies," and the Soviet Navy draws freely from the mercantile pool whenever it is in the interests of the fighting services. *Jane's* summarizes, "The Soviet Navy has reached out to all the oceans of the world."

All the Russian firsts in space, beginning with the Sputnik on October 5, 1957, testify to the extent and quality of Soviet research. The United States still has not been able to produce a rocket with a thrust equivalent to that of the Russians.

Undoubtedly, the Soviet economy is also paying a price for that country's diversion of research facilities and efforts to the military field. The expansion of the Soviet military and space programs has preempted a large share of the high-quality men, machinery, materials and thinking that otherwise might have been used for modernizing industry and agriculture. Perhaps this explains why the Russian growth rate in the output of all goods and services has dropped from an impressive 7.1 per cent a year during the 1950's to about 5.3 per cent per year since 1960.

Of course, the Soviet Union is not lacking in the quantity and quality of conventional armaments which are part and parcel of the accoutrements of a first-class fighting force. The massive land armies of its allies further augment the strength of the Warsaw Pact bloc.

So much for the overwhelming might of the two atomic colossi malevolently eyeing each other across a trembling world. But we have not yet exhausted the rollcall of the military power that has been mustered on our tiny planet. Behind the bamboo curtain lurks a third mammoth threat to the security of the world.

With the detonation of a hydrogen bomb and the testing of a nuclear-tipped missile over a distance of a few hundred miles, Red China has signalled its coming of age in the arms race. The Chinese People's Liberation Army of 2.7 million, with 2-2.5 million men in the ground forces, 75,000-100,000 in the air force, 135,000 in the navy, and the remainder in militarized border guard units, is the largest in the world. Arsenals at Mukden and elsewhere are equipping the Chinese army with modern effective infantry weapons—rifles, machine guns, bazookas, mines, grenades, automatic and semi-automatic weapons, mortars, light rocket launchers, recoilless rifles, and light and medium artillery. Worn-out Russian tanks, trucks, heavy artillery pieces and aircraft are being replaced with Chinese-made types or copies.

China boasts the third largest air force, with 3,500 planes, mostly MIG 15's and 17's. China can produce both of these models, as well as MIG 19's and is working on production of the supersonic MIG 21's. In addition, China is reputed to have 400 light jet bomber IL-28's and 100 propeller driven TU-4 bombers capable of carrying nuclear bombs.

It is estimated that the arms budget of Red China totals $6 billion per year, equal to that of Great Britain, and the fourth highest in the world.

In addition to the regular People's Liberation Army, there is a People's Armed Police of about 500,000 men under the control of the Ministry of Internal Security. Finally, under the slogan "Every man a soldier," militia units have been formed in virtually every factory and commune. Jenmin Jih Pao and other newspapers carry frequent reports of major maneuvers by units of militia men and women under warlike conditions. A program of defense sports for boys and girls includes bayonet practice, target shooting, grenade throwing and marching. The Chinese militia may consist of as many as 200 million people. Of course, it need hardly have been mentioned that the United States, Russia and most other countries also have trained reserves that number in the millions.

Allied with Red China is the People's Army of North Vietnam with a regular force of about 480,000 men with a million more in the ready reserve, and North Korea with approximately equal strength.

Among the so-called uncommitted nations, not aligned with any of these major blocs, we can count many more millions of men under arms. For example, India's armed strength is put at close to one million (with $1.67 billion of this poverty stricken country's budget of $5.55 billion earmarked for defense), Indonesia's at 350,000, Pakistan's at 250,000, Israel's at 250,000, and the United Arab Republic at 130,000.

The pot is kept stirred and boiling by the persistent merchants of death who are still peddling their obscene wares. Private American defense industries and arms merchants ship over $1 billion in military exports annually with credit guaranteed by the government. Samuel Cummings, founder of the International Armaments Corporation, the world's leading private seller of arms, commented, "You get rather cynical in this business." The United States government itself is one of the most active arms merchandisers with sales amounting to $1.5 billion a year. The United States has sold arms impartially to Israel and the United Arab Republic, Greece and Turkey, India and Pakistan "to advance peace and stability." It was disclosed that 25 per cent of the loans made by the Export-Import Bank, originally created to aid trade, were used to finance this business. Over $600 million was secret Country X loans to underdeveloped countries. All this was motivated by the laudable need to counter the Communist threat, secure American employment and profit, and ease the gold drain.

The Soviet Union contributes its bit with military sales of about $400 million a year. West Germany, France, Britain, Sweden, and other countries are active in both the private industry and government sectors of arms merchandising. Labor Britain even appointed a supersalesman to push the sale of British arms—shades of Basil Zaharoff.

Add to this merchandising the more than $33 billion

worth of arms donated in military assistance grants by the United States to sixty-four countries in the fifteen years since 1950. In addition, the Soviet Union, Red China, France and Britain, among other countries, have extensive military aid programs whereby arms grants are made to allied nations (actual or wishful). Thus, for instance, the Soviet Union aids Algeria, Egypt, Syria and Somalia while the United States assists Morocco, Israel and Ethopia. The scope of this illegal gun running was accidentally revealed in May, 1965, when Kenya intercepted seventy-five tons of Chinese arms being convoyed to Uganda.

The Red Chinese atomic detonations near remote Lob Nor, in the Taklamakan Desert in the central Asian province of Sinkiang, dramatize the most serious peril—the sword of Damocles—hanging over our age, the proliferation of atomic weapons. Some, like Lord Chalfont, Roswell Gilpatric and the late Robert F. Kennedy, feel that this problem of proliferation is a more urgent crisis than flare-ups in the world's current trouble spots.

The entry of Red China into the nuclear club, for instance, creates ripples of fear and tension in countries such as India, Japan, and Pakistan, thus, generating internal pressure on each of these governments to get into the nuclear arms race. After all, the measuring rod of the stature and prestige of a people has become possession of atomic weapons, and this will not change, anti-proliferation treaty or no. Remember the psychological blow to British prestige when the Skybolt project was scrapped.

Besides, nuclear technology is advancing so rapidly that the cost of building a minimum nuclear capability is decreasing dramatically each year. Now that the ultra-centrifuge process provides a relatively inexpensive way for separating uranium 235 from Uranium 238, the price tag for an atomic bomb is unbelievably cheap. Dr. Homi J. Bhabha, the late chairman of India's Atomic Energy Commission, estimated that India could achieve a ten kiloton explosion for an expenditure of about 1.75 million rupees ($368,000) and a 2 megaton explosion for about three million rupees ($630,000). This increasing economic feasibility of nuclear power is bringing more and more countries within reach of nuclear capability.

The United States Arms Control and Disarmament Agency lists twenty countries with sufficient technical sophistication to build a nuclear bomb. These are Belgium, Canada, Czechoslovakia, East Germany, West Germany, India, Italy, Japan, Switzerland, the Netherlands, Norway, Poland, Romania, Spain, Israel, the United Arab Republic, Mexico, Indonesia, Pakistan and South Africa.

Power reactors, already operating or under construction, according to the London Institute of Strategic Studies, will produce enough Plutonium to make 236 bombs a year in India and progressively smaller numbers in Canada, West Germany, Italy, Japan, Belgium, Sweden, Czechoslovakia, down to a mere ten in the Netherlands. Israel, Egypt, Switzerland and Norway could produce fewer than ten bombs annually from their stores.

Such nuclear proliferation will re-create the chaos of King Arthur's last battle at Camlon. The reader will remember that the forces of King Arthur and of his rebellious son Modred had gathered on the field of Camlon to negotiate an end to their warring. One of the gathered knights, being stung by an asp, drew his sword to kill the reptile. The great legendary King of Britain was mortally wounded in the slaughter that ensued.

With the power of decision over the use of nuclear

weapons widely dispersed all over the map, the atomic arsenals of the secondary nations will function as a wick to ignite the powder kegs of the major thermonuclear powers and set off chain reactions of devastation. With nuclear spread, an attacked nation will be unable to evaluate where the attack came from and what it means. Since the surviving forces would have to respond instantly in order not to be destroyed by follow-up waves of the attack, the only result would have to be the loosing of atomic firepower indiscriminately in all directions. The power to provoke a catalytic, all-out war, either deliberately or through clumsiness, would thus pass into the hands of the less responsible third countries.

President Kennedy stated, in his broadcast of July 28, 1963, marking his signature of the partial test ban treaty, "I ask you to stop and think for a moment what it would mean to have nuclear weapons in many hands—in the hands of countries large and small, stable and unstable, responsible and irresponsible, scattered throughout the world. There would be no rest for anyone then, no stability, no real security, and no chance of effective disarmament. There would only be increased chances of accidental war, and an increased necessity for the great powers to involve themselves in otherwise local conflicts."

Our peace of mind is not eased by the prediction that the advanced type of nuclear bombs exploded by the Chinese would indicate the production of an operational hydrogen warhead before 1970. If thermonuclear bombs become so easy to manufacture, it is fair to predict that the other powers on the threshold of nuclear weapons will possess these bombs in the not too distant future. What then?

Suppose the Martians were to dispatch the proverbial spy to report back on the state of the earth. He would find wide variations in topography from sea to mountain to desert to plain; extremes in climate; endless species of animal and plant life; polyglot languages, faces, races, shapes, clothing, mores among the people of the planet. He would find all gradations and degradations of governments and economic systems. He would even have to report oases of affluence and learning in the general pattern of hunger, disease and illiteracy.

There is only one thing that our spy will find everywhere—the soldier and his gun. The New York *Herald Tribune* of April 2, 1966, carried photographs of Marshal Rodion Malinovsky reporting to the Communist Party Congress and of General Lyman Lemnitzer reporting to President Johnson. Each is bedecked in full military regalia and festooned with decorations.

Nothing is more universal, more characteristic, more illustrative of the life of man on this planet than this posture of war. Imagine a whole world, a whole "civilization," an entire culture concentrated upon the mad demand for the most perfect methods of slaughter. Imagine a whole world worshipping the Moloch of militarism—"the destroyer of youth, the raper of women, the annihilator of the best in the race, the very mower of life."

Even the Japanese, who disavowed resort to force in their Constitution, maintain a military establishment of 171,000 in the ground forces, 39,000 in the air force and 33,000 in the fleet. This so-called Japanese Self-Defense Force is provided with a $1 billion budget.

We must face the fact that the image of this world is one of a garrison state, armed to the teeth, conscripted for war, mobilized on a hair-trigger alert for war, organized for war, dedicated to war, grounded in war, destined for war, fearful of war. Test this picture against the facts of the newly emerging nations. What is the first task which such a nation undertakes? Does it build roads or hospitals or schools? Of course not, it builds an army. Millions of men under arms are marching, carrying rifles, throwing grenades, shouting slogans of hate, only waiting for the command to commence fire.

We should not be surprised. A state of war or preparedness for war has been the normal condition of mankind since before the dawn of recorded history. Fighting has always been and may, in all probability, always be the ultimate occupation of man. The only thing that has changed is the casualty potential. Ten million were killed and twenty million maimed in World War I; thirty-three million were killed and thirty-five million maimed in World War II; no less than one billion will be killed and hundreds of millions maimed in the first exchange of Nuclear War I.

After all, the subject matter of disarmament is arms. Before we can discuss disarmament, it is important to understand the scope and dimension of the program of militarization which holds this earth in an iron grip. It is important to recognize that our world's everyday life is based and grounded on war and preparation for war. The world—this house we live in—is dedicated to the gods of war and, to that end, it is stacked from basement to attic with cords of dynamite. The human beings who inhabit that world are allowed barely sufficient room in which to move carefully and gingerly amid the stacked explosive power.

So, good-night, sweet citizen. Sleep well in your house tonight. Pleasant dreams.

3

The Great Deterrent

Good morning. We were lucky again last night and we are still here to tell the tale. Well, perhaps today . . . or tonight . . . or tomorrow. One is reminded of the French practice, only recently abandoned, of not informing the condemned of the exact date of his execution. Thus the prisoner would go to bed each night never knowing if it would be his last. The reader might even recall the movie, *We Are All Murderers* which dealt with this subject. There is no more exquisite form of torture.

Silly children, our leaders will say—frightened out of your wits and scared half to death by a gallimaufry of hobgoblins and paper tigers. Now, you know very well, they will say, that this mountain of arms was accumulated for defense, and defense only, just as was done before 1939, before 1914, and before every other war in history.

You also know very well, they will continue, that this mountain of arms was accumulated for the express purpose of not using it—just as it was not for use before 1939, before 1914, and before every other war in history.

It is certainly furthest from our minds to use this force to kill anyone. Did not President Kennedy declare, "We increase our arms at a heavy cost, primarily to make certain we will never use them."

Don't pay any attention to ex-Secretary McNamara when he said, "We have spent $2 billion to strengthen our nuclear deterrent and to strengthen it in a way that would enable us to use it immediately. It is absurd to think that we would have unbalanced the budget simply to strengthen a weapon that we had decided never to use under any circumstances." He is merely throwing a sop to the military.

The citizen can only shake his head at this great puzzlement. Is this threat of annihilation—this threat which is enforced by over 300,000 megatons of nuclear firepower —only an act, a pantomime, a charade? After all, our leaders are not all stupid or insane and one must give them due credit for adequate knowledge and ability in the performance of their jobs. There must be a certain amount of logic in their seeming madness.

This logic goes by the name of the theory of deterrence. Now this, too, is a new name for a very old doctrine that goes back to the dawn of recorded history. In more classical times, it was known as the para bellum doctrine. Supposedly it was the advice given to the Emperor Theodosius by Vegetius: "Si vis pacem para bellum." "If you desire peace, prepare for war." President Washington repeated this advice in his first annual message to the Congress. "To be prepared for war is one of the most effectual means of preserving peace."

Now the theory of deterrence is a subtle doctrine which is difficult to define and explain. It is a mosaic of precarious little details and glib assumptions. Essentially, it is a psychological process whereby good (or more accurately, rational) behavior is forced upon our adversaries through the fear of their self destruction. The basic theory involves the use of latent power to constrain the other fellow to behave under the threat of using this force if, and when, necessary. If each side clearly has the capability to turn the other into a nuclear wasteland, neither is likely to initiate nuclear war: so the argument goes.

While loudly and continuously professing its intention not to use this force, the deterrer then proceeds to build and maintain a credible arms establishment that is second to none. Then-Major General Curtis E. Le May best described this force in testimony before the United States Senate Subcommittee on the Air Force of the Eighty-fourth Congress: "A deterrent force is one that is large enough and sufficient enough that no matter what the enemy force does, either offensively or defensively, he still will receive a quantity of bombs or explosive force that is more than he is willing to accept. Therefore, he never starts a war."

Robert McNamara explained the proposition as follows to the House Armed Services Committee on February 18, 1965: "The strategic objectives of our general nuclear war forces are to deter a deliberate nuclear attack upon the United States and its allies by maintaining a clear and convincing capability to inflict unacceptable damage on an attacker, even were that attacker to strike first."

Thus, the two requirements of a deterrent policy are (a) a credible force and (b) the communication to an adversary of the willingness to use at the proper time whatever portion of that force may be necessary. In the words of General Earle G. Wheeler, Chairman of the Joint Chiefs of Staff, "Deterrence is a combination of weapons and a state of mind."

Now, at the same time that the United States is building and maintaining that credible force and is communicating *its* willingness to use it, the Soviet Union (and, to a lesser degree, other nations) is building and maintaining that credible force and is communicating *its* willingness to use it.

So perhaps deterrence can best be defined as a delicate calibrated balancing act, with the fears of mutual annihilation the balance. Perhaps that is why the doctrine is sometimes called stabilized deterrence. In the same way that the Hague Convention had maintained the peace before 1914 and the League of Nations had maintained the peace before 1939, thus is the United Nations maintaining the peace today. In the same way that the balance of power and collective security maintained the peace before 1914 and 1939, a more grim and terrible force is maintaining the peace today.

That force is the balance of terror in the form of nuclear weapons. In the same way that the bow and arrow and the spear and dynamite and the rifle and the machine gun and the tank and the bomber had proscribed war in previous ages, thus has the existence of weapons of massive destruction, in the form of atomic bombs, outlawed war in our generation. We have achieved peace through mutual terror. In the inimitable words of Sir Winston Churchill, "by a process of sublime irony, the world would reach a stage where safety will be the sturdy child of terror and survival the twin brother of annihilation."

In 1910, Norman Angell wrote about the "Great Illusion" of another era. Now, a new illusion is being welcomed: with tension increasing, with the poker chips being flung on the table by the fistful, with everything piling up, we have finally arrived at an acknowledged stalemate—a cozy old balance of power. This could well be the last illusion.

But can a perpetual balance be maintained upon the knife edge of mutual nuclear suicide? John J. McCloy, disarmament adviser to President Kennedy, has stated, "A nice balance of deterrents, even if it ever could be attained, is a rather slender reed on which to rest for long." An uncontrolled, unpredictable arms race is constantly threatening to throw out of balance by each new weapon the frightfully perilous equilibrium.

Further, each international adventure, such as the introduction of Soviet missiles into Cuba, or the introduction of American power into North Vietnam, threatens to destroy the precarious teetering balance.

Besides, how can the leader of any nation be satisfied with the strength of his country when the enemy's power to cancel this capability continues apace? He dares not fall behind. He must assume the worst plausible case yet; he must always be certain that enough missiles will survive to wipe out the enemy, even after absorbing a surprise attack. Only as long as the enemy is convinced of this capability will it be rationally deterred from initiating a nuclear war, and thereby risking national suicide.

The determination of a balance of deterrent is not an exact mathematical calculation. Professor Hans Morganthau has pointed out that this uncertainty of all power calculations makes the balance of power incapable of all practical application and leads to its very negation in practice. Since no leader can be sure that his calculation of the distribution of power at any particular moment in the history of his nation is correct, he must err on the safe side and at least make sure that, whatever errors he may commit, these miscalculations will not put his nation at a disadvantage in the contest for power.

Thus, the leader must strive to have at least a margin of safety which will allow him to make erroneous calculations and still maintain the balance of terror. To that effect, all leaders actively engaged in the international struggle for power must actually aim not at a balance, or equality of power, but at a superiority of power for his nation. There is an irresistible temptation to add still another safety factor to the national arsenal. Since no man can foresee how large his miscalculation will turn out to be, all leaders must ultimately seek the maximum of power obtainable under the circumstances.

Neither side can ever stop adding to the firepower of its nuclear stockpile, because the entire system of deterrence is based upon the goal of having the larger atomic force to begin with, so as to have more left for purposes of retaliation after attack. Further, each nation ends up by running an arms race with itself because the idea that the other side *might* get weapon X has the same impact as if the enemy *actually* had weapon X.

This is precisely the conclusion reached by reporter Daniel Lang, who wandered through the maze of Washington, D.C., in elucidation of what he called "An Inquiry into Enoughness." Notebook in hand, he asked generals, scientists, diplomats and statesmen, "Since we already have thousands of nuclear weapons, when will we have enough?" The only answer he received was "dilemma and paradox." He even found an inter-service rivalry based upon acquiring atomic weapons as status symbols. Lang repeated his pilgrimage, journeying to other capitals of the world. He still received no answer.

There is another balance involved in deterrence—a balance of risks. There has been no intent here to imply that peace by deterrence has created an idyllic state of peace and tranquility. That would be entirely too much to expect from the present status quo where two armed camps sit glaring menacingly at each other. That would be entirely too much to expect from a world evidently split into hostile, implacable camps with each side entrenching itself and its ideology ever deeper into the accustomed military rut. Perhaps it would be more accurate to depict peace by deterrence as a great beast of prey, temporarily shackled by the nuclear-weapons stalemate, who is struggling desperately to break its bonds.

It would be unreasonable constantly to brandish the threat of nuclear retaliation and, at the same time, to assume it would never be necessary to carry it out. The war for which the nations prepare so as not to have to fight it, although sometimes called impossible, is possible just the same. If it were indeed physically or morally impossible, deterrence would cease to operate.

Thus, peace by deterrence is, at most, only a partial and relative peace. Actually, scarcely a day has passed since V-J Day, 1945, during which men have not died in conflict. They have made the supreme sacrifice by the thousands in Greece, Israel, Kashmir, Ladakh, Malaysia, Suez, Korea, the Congo, Vietnam, Algeria, Laos, Cyprus, and many other places on the globe.

In the same manner, men were dying and training and preparing for total war before 1914 in Manchuria, the Balkans, the Philippines, South Africa, China, Turkey, Mexico, and elsewhere; and before 1939 in Russia, Siberia, India, Manchuria, China, Spain, Ethiopia, Albania, and elsewhere.

With each nation in a posture of war, it is incumbent upon its adversaries to spy out the armor and position of any possible opponent. Hence, we have U-2 planes, observation satellites, photographic reconnaissance, border incursions, plain old-fashioned cloak and dagger espionage, and all the other pinprick provocations of this age of deterrence.

In addition to spying out whatever armor the enemy might have in place, it is also necessary to continuously test and probe the resolute maintenance of the second requirement of a posture of deterrence, namely, the firm will and resolve of the enemy to use the armor. It is well that our leaders can keep the military equipment and men busy in these activities (with an occasional brushfire war thrown in for good measure). Otherwise, how could they justify to their people the extortion of ever more billions in taxes and the drafting of ever more millions of our youth. Such sacrifices cannot be inspired by rusting armor and idling men.

Nor can you build up a standing army and then throw it back into a box like tin soldiers. Armies, equipped to the teeth with highly developed instruments of murder, generate their own momentum. There must be an enemy and a peril even if these apparitions have to be conjured up in order to hone the combat readiness of the masses. The Defense Ministries understand that they must keep their electorates in a constant state of semi-terror in order to justify their extravagances.

Naturally, these activities involve a certain amount of competition in calculated risk taking. If one side is unwilling to risk global war, while the other side is willing to risk such a conflagration, then the side which is willing to run the risk will be triumphant in all negotiations and will ultimately reduce the other side to complete impotence. In the words of Secretary McNamara, "We know that a nuclear holocaust would be a disaster of unimaginable proportions, but we know also that unless we are prepared to place everything at risk, we cannot hope to save anything from disaster."

Joseph Alsop tells the story that President Kennedy risked the destruction of the United States during the October 1962 Cuban missile crisis when he thought the odds that the Russians were *not* bluffing were "somewhere between one in three and even odds." It should be made clear here that President Kennedy, in risking the destruction of the United States, was not primarily concerned with the military threat of the Soviet missiles. Theodore Sorensen, in his book *Kennedy*, discloses that the President was more concerned about the *appearance* of a change in the strategic balance than about any *actual* one. He was more worried about the global political balance and the possibility of a major humiliation in the Cold War as a result of the confrontation.

Perhaps now we can understand why deterrence is also called "Brinkmanship." In the words of President Eisenhower, "After all, brinkmanship is absolutely necessary to keep the peace. . . . It is something you do to show you are not going to sacrifice a single vital interest of the United

States." Thus, to protect the peace a nation must always appear willing to advance to the brink of war.

The inevitable result of nuclear brinkmanship, nuclear gambles, nuclear dares is a state of continuous tension. More than once has mankind hung between hell and heaven. More than once has mankind looked down the gun barrel of nuclear war into the pit of the inferno. Will we be lucky enough to step back from the brink again after the next confrontation? In the words of President Kennedy, after the Cuban crisis, "You can't have too many of these."

One begins to comprehend why Professor Seymour Melman described the method of deterrence as political-psychological, rather than military. No matter how powerful or overwhelming a nation's military capability may be, its physical and material effectiveness will count as nothing unless that nation can show its willingness to face up to the risks of Armageddon. Each side must show that it has burned its bridges so that it cannot retreat. Deterrence is achieved when one side's readiness to run risks in relation to the other is high; it is least effective when the willingness to run risks is low.

Behind the incredible complexity and sophistication of the world of nuclear weapons and their delivery systems, the doctrine of deterrence (and the cold war which it has spawned) comes down to a test as to whether the free world or the communist world displays greater purposefulness and toughness of fiber. The heart of a credible deterrent in a nuclear age lies in being prepared to face the consequences should deterrence fail.

The question arises whether deterrence means the prevention of nuclear war or only its discouragement up to that point (sooner or later inevitable) at which it must take place.

It turns out, then, that we are not making weapons; we are making psychology. The tens upon tens of billions of defense dollars have been spent in the most lavish experiment in behavioral science that the world has ever seen. This chip-on-the-shoulder attitude that is labelled deterrence is really a war of nerves: of bluster, bluff and belligerence. The theory and practice of the great deterrence has become the thory and practice of the great bluff.

For instance, the reader will remember that it was proposed, during the Cuban missile crisis of October, 1962, that the United States show its good faith by dismantling its own missile sites in Turkey and Italy. The Administration rejected this suggestion out of hand. It was later revealed by a member of the Cabinet, Douglas Dillon, that the Jupiter missiles at these foreign bases were really obsolescent, of little value, and had just about been forced on Turkey and Italy.

Now, each minute of each day, each side is trying to force the other to back down. At the same time, each is pretending that nothing can make it give ground and that it will consider war seriously if the other side does not back down. Each minute of each day, each side must try desperately to pierce the bluff and pretense of the other side and to evaluate the seriousness of its nerve and will as matched against its own.

The worst of all situations could thus result if one side underestimated the seriousness of the resolve of the other side. Suppose side A had enough resolve and knew it had enough resolve, but suppose, for some reason, side B did not believe this and so provoked side A so that A was forced to initiate a war in retaliation.

Secretary McNamara touched on this same possibility in his often-quoted commencement address at the University of Michigan in Ann Arbor, on June 16, 1962. He said, "The mere fact that no nation could rationally take steps leading to a nuclear war does not guarantee that a nuclear war cannot take place. Not only do nations sometimes act in ways that are hard to explain on a rational basis, but even when acting in a rational way they sometimes, indeed disturbingly often, act on the basis of misunderstandings of the true facts of a situation. They misjudge the way others will react and the way others will interpret what they are doing." Charles Yost's law of disproportionate response to miscalculated challenges still operates.

Remember the cartoon by Don Wright in the *Miami News*: Two battered survivors crawl out of two giant craters to confront each other. The caption reads, "You mean you were bluffing?"

A prime example of this situation is the Japanese overreaching attack upon Pearl Harbor. How could any psychiatrist explain what deluded General Hideki Tojo and his warlords, who were strictly bush leaguers, into believing that they could effectively play in the big leagues? Nobutaka Ike addressed himself to this question in *Japan's Decision for War: Records of the 1941 Policy Conferences*. Was Japan's bizarre miscalculation of America's response to military attack inspired by the memory of the Russo-Japanese War of 1905? Or did it indicate a streak of fatalism among the Japanese leaders? How could the Russians have so grossly miscalculated the relative Israeli and Arab strengths in the Six-Day War of June 1967?

Given the absence of any direct, meaningful communication between the United States and Red China, what are the possibilities of the miscalculation by one side of the motives of the other? How can we be sure that the signals are being read correctly?

What happens if deterrence fails is that each side is prepared to exterminate the entire population of its opponent and to have its own population exterminated in retaliation or through the backlash of fallout. The nation that uses atomic weapons becomes subject to the fate of a bee: when it stings it must inevitably perish, for having made use of its sting. To quote former Secretary Mc-Namara: "The blunt fact is, then, that neither the Soviet Union nor the United States can attack the other without being destroyed in retaliation." Sic transit deterrer and deterred.

Given the tremendous growth of the present weapons systems, it is very difficult for either side to form an accurate judgment of the will and resolve of the other side. There is always the possibility that the opponent's will might have become paralyzed through the contemplation of the enormity of the resulting human catastrophe. It follows that as the power of modern weapons grows, the threat of an all-out war loses its credibility because the mind of man is repulsed and revolted by the consequences. Of course, a deterrent which one is afraid to implement when it is challenged ceases to be a deterrent.

In this macabre game of brandishing threats which

only a madman could unleash it becomes preferable for the statesman to act the madman. How else could he be taken seriously?

In order to guard against the danger that one's will and resolve might be underestimated, the inevitable tendency is to push the theory of deterrence to its ultimate of total annihilation in infinitesimal time. The time available to make the most terrible decisions is being inhumanly compressed to the point where the response becomes automatic. Then, once the reprisal is set off automatically, a possible aggressor knows that neither political expediency nor betrayal nor moral constraint nor fear of additional punishment can paralyze the will. Retaliation, perhaps posthumous retaliation, is assured.

This ultimate, logical—and inevitable—end to the theory of the deterrent is the doomsday machine. It is a clockwork mechanism, buried thousands of feet underground in some uninhabited wasteland, which is connected to a computer which is in turn connected by a reliable communication system to thousands of sensory devices all over the country. The computer is programmed so that if the country is hit with a predetermined level of force, the device is triggered and retaliation is automatically launched untouched by human hand or brain or will or command. The device, once set, brooks no intervention and its operation is as automatic as the movement of the hours and of the heavens. The gap between an invulnerable deterrent and a vulnerable population grows ever wider. The reader will be pleased to know that Dr. Herman Kahn estimates that a doomsday machine could be built by 1970 for a cost well under $100 billion.

This is the point: the theory of deterrence contains no

provision for its own resolution. It offers no end and no solution. If the effectiveness of the deterrent resides precisely in its certainty and its horror, any attempt to reduce either the certainty or the horror will reduce the power to deter. Man is trapped in a vise of protracted conflict; he is condemned to wander forever in the nuclear jungle. Nuclear materials don't go away or disappear; they pile higher and higher. President Kennedy stated, "Only when our arms are sufficient beyond doubt can we be certain beyond doubt that they will never be employed." The point is that arms can never be sufficient beyond doubt. The rat race must continue on and on and on, without a finish line. The race ends only when all the contestants are dead.

Nor does deterrence come cheap. The United States alone is spending upwards of $15 billion a year on its nuclear weapons in order to present a reasonable façade of credibility. That is the peculiar feature of credibility. It cannot be achieved in just an adequate, limited fashion at bargain prices. Last year's styles or models just will not do. Only the newest, latest, most expensive weapons will serve to maintain a nation's credibility and standing in the exclusive nuclear club.

Who is in charge of this game of atomic roulette which we are playing, with the lives of the peoples of the world wagered as stakes? It should not come as a shock in this Alice in Wonderland script that the croupier is the military. What more titillating paradox can we find than to discover that our men of war are conducting the quest for peace through deterrence?

Who pays heed any more to the sage advice offered by George Washington in his Farewell Address: "Hence likewise they will avoid the necessity of those overgrown Military Establishments which under any form of government are inauspicious to liberty, and which are regarded as particularly hostile to Republican Liberty?" The probability is that the Military Establishment will conquer the United States long before the Communists have an opportunity to launch their attack. At one time, war was war and peace was peace. War belonged to the military and peace to the civilians. After a war was over, the country reverted to the people, and the military's prestige, budgets and glory shrank accordingly. Now, the distinction between war and peace has become blurred. It is no longer the state that has an army; it is the army that has captivated the nation.

No doubt the military training manual has been revised so that conscripts are no longer taught to hate and kill with weapons and vengeance. Instead, the Sermon on the Mount has been substituted and the men are trained to turn the other cheek. Love your enemies, bless them that curse you and pray for them that despitefully use you. In fact, the motto of the Strategic Air Command is, "Peace is our profession." One is reminded of George Orwell.

Does any other kind of training make sense when the primary objective of the military force is to deter war? As General Pierre Gallois has put it, "From now on it must no longer be a matter of carrying out combat operations, but of renouncing battle altogether. The best general staff is no longer the one which has best prepared its country to carry out operations, but the one which has been able to indoctrinate the futility and the dangers of a trial by force."

Armed with this description, it is feared that one would not be able to identify a single general staff or a single military establishment. Unfortunately, none has renounced battle and none has adopted the Sermon on the Mount as its manual. To the military, the prospect of disarmament is frightening. Instead, they are seeking to prepare continuously for that momentous day when the constant probing will disclose that Achilles heel, that break in the solid wall of the enemy's defense, which will enable their forces to pour through the breach to glory. As far as the armed forces of any nation are concerned, their business is still murder as usual except that the scale has become more wholesale. The function of the military is to kill; it cannot live except through murder.

As proof, witness the case of Second Lieutenant Henry Howe who was sentenced to two years' imprisonment at hard labor for taking part in an anti-war demonstration, although he was off duty and in civilian clothes. Or, take the case of Seaman James Gilbert who was sentenced to 30 days at hard labor for wearing the inverted Y in a circle peace symbol.

As a matter of fact, under the conditions of instant preparedness that are required by the strategy of deterrence there has been an even greater devolution of authority upon the military. By making the deterrent the principal instrument of foreign policy, its direction has inevitably been placed in the hands of the general staffs, with civilian government and diplomacy becoming more and more subservient to the military policy.

Until that glorious day of the coming of the Messiah, the fact will remain that armies acquire arms not to prevent wars but to win them. In the words of General

Douglas A. MacArthur, "In war there is no substitute for victory." To the soldier, the ultimate evil is not to fight a war, but to lose it. Yes, the generals, on all sides, are still thinking in terms not only of war, but of something called victory. And as long as generals believe that victory can be won, war cannot be dismissed as unthinkable. Correction: the preferred word is not "victory" any more; now it is called "prevailing" or "favorable settlement."

United States Air Force General Sidney F. Griffin—who was Director of the Office of Information and Education of the Defense Department from 1957 to 1960 and later became associated with one of the brain trust institutes—wrote, "The best way of discouraging an implacable enemy from war—any kind of war—is to be in a position to win, to survive handily and to act with confidence of this position."

General Dwight D. Eisenhower advised the Army War College, "You must make sure that if such a [nuclear] war occurs, that at least we are not the nation most seriously damaged."

Then-Deputy Secretary of Defense Roswell Gilpatrick stated on December 21, 1961, "If forceful interference with our rights and obligations should lead to violent conflict—as well it might—the United States does not intend to be defeated."

Ex-Chairman of the Joint Chiefs of Staff Admiral Radford declared, "I demand total victory over the Communist system, not stalemate."

One-time Air Force Chief General Nathan Twining said, "If it were not for the politicians, I would settle the war by bombing Russia."

General Curtis LeMay would have ended the Vietnamese war in a hurry by bombing factories, road junctions, docks, oil tanks and industrial complexes until North Vietnam was blasted back "into the Stone Age."

Robert Strausz-Hupé, a top adviser to the Defense Department, contends that there are certain minimum objectives which the United States must seek to obtain even at the risk of general nuclear war. These minimum objectives are security of the North American base, maintenance of Free World positions around the Sino-Soviet bloc, and control of seaways, airways and outer space. For the attainment of these minimum ends, a war is thinkable in the opinion of Mr. Strausz-Hupé.

The military want war: that is their profession and career. Mussolini's son, after dropping a load of bombs on Ethiopia, was struck with the beauty of the burst below. Capt. Thomas S. Roberts grinned and said "Hot Damn" when he shot down a MIG-17 jet fighter over North Vietnam. The fact that men were dying in the process was only incidental. One wonders whether Capt. Roberts, or the younger Mussolini, had ever read Walt Whitman: "For my enemy is dead, a man divine as myself is dead." At the same time, Major Claude R. Eatherly, who expressed remorse over his role in the Hiroshima bombing, was declared insane and committed. One is reminded of Siegfried Sassoon in World War I.

Herman Kahn, who is certainly not a woolly-headed peace agitator, concludes, "In the long run, a purely military approach to the security problem can lead to disaster for civilization and by long run, I mean decades, not centuries." It does not seem to matter that a nuclear war would be so destructive of human, material and moral values as to render victory indistinguishable from defeat.

Nobody wins a suicide pact. One can almost see the generals rubbing their palms in anticipation of the military orgy the next time.

By this time, the beauty of this system of deterrence, which promises all things to all men, must have dawned upon the reader in the same way that the truth was perceived by the condemned in Kafka's *Penal Colony*. This cornucopia horn of plenty that is deterrence showers its bounty on all: offering to the worker good jobs with overtime pay; to the businessman inflated profits; to the scholar lavish research grants; to the statesman public adulation as he careens from crisis to crisis; to the military men medals and promotions and ultimate power. Only a spoilsport, like Friedrich Duerrenmatt in his *Visit*, would point to the figure of death waiting in the shadows to reap his ultimate and inevitable harvest.

> We have made a covenant with death
> And with hell are we at agreement.
>
> ISAIAH

4

The Computer Takes Over

Of course, continuation of the peace enforced by deterrence—and continuation of the lives of the peoples of the world—presupposes that decisions will invariably be made in a rational fashion by objectively informed political and military leaders. Advocates of the balance of terror deterrent must logically make the assumption that the awesome power of the atom will be exercised by these leaders with responsibility and restraint. Former Premier Khrushchev phrased the proposition in his own earthy manner: "We do not want a war, not because we are afraid but because we have a head and brains and therefore know what a war means."

Here is another great puzzlement for the citizen. We in the West are told that the vast structure of armaments, which backstops the theory of deterrence, is necessary to contain the mad dogs of communism who cannot be trusted and who are straining at the leash to overrun the free world. The people in the East are told that the pile of arms is necessary to restrain the mad dogs of imperialism who cannot be trusted and who are straining at the leash to subjugate the socialist camp. In the face of all this suspicion, it would appear that each camp, under the theory of deterrence, is reposing the highest form of trust on the reasonableness of the other. Each night the citizens of each camp sleep well only because they entrust their lives to the nuclear prudence of their bitterest enemies.

There would seem to be at least two other fallacies in this presupposition of rationality. First, a difference of opinion might conceivably exist between the leaders of different countries as to what course of action they think prudent and sane. Herman Kahn, the high strategist of deterrence, even contends that "depending on the circumstances and the alternatives which a nation has, it is quite possible that decision makers could rationally and sanely choose to go to war."

The other criticism asserts that a program of deterrence assumes a degree of human rationality for which history offers absolutely no warranty. J. B. Priestly states, "Surely, it is the wildest idealism, at the furthest remove from a sober realism, to assume that men will always behave reasonably in line with their best interests. Yet this is precisely what we are asked to believe and to stake our all on it." And wasn't it Mark Twain who remarked that his experiments had proven to him that man is the "Unreasoning Animal"? "Note his history . . . It seems plain to me that whatever he is he is not a reasoning animal. His record is the fantastic record of a maniac."

A most bizarre anomaly must have occurred to the reader at this point. We argue vociferously that disarmament won't work because we can't trust the Russians. Yet, we stake our lives under the theory of deterrence in the trust that the Russians will react rationally. No one seems to suggest that total disarmament with inspection eliminates the need for trusting the enemy.

It is plain to see, then, that there is a high degree of risk implicit in the doctrine of deterrence. As Herman Kahn puts it, "When one competes in risk taking, one is taking risks. If one takes risks, one may be unlucky and lose the gamble." But there is no cause for anxiety or undue alarm on the part of the citizen. Dr. Kahn and the other scholar-strategists of deterrence have charted the course down to the last kiloton and casualty.

The trick in this competition in risk taking is to calculate the location of two very fine lines. For the nation which is paying the bills, the men who shape strategy must figure the devastation threshold beneath which recourse to force can be considered profitable, and above which it is wiser to withhold the megatons. Simultaneously, for any possible adversaries, the analyst must find the ignition or flash point beyond which any further provocation or irritation would trigger nuclear retaliation. Sometimes, the calculations go awry as in the instance where the Red Chinese entered the Korean War against the prediction of both the IBM machines and the generals; or where computer intelligence led to original assumptions that the Vietnam war could be won without a massive United States effort. But the calculations must be made.

To that end, giant research organizations, "think factories," have been formed to assist the various governments in military analysis. Two of the largest in the United States are Dr. Kahn's Hudson Institute and the Rand Corporation. The latter, which has been called the "American Academy of Death and Destruction," holds research contracts totaling $23 million annually, and boasts a staff of 1168 military intellectuals with no less than 280 Ph.D's. The respectable high priests of civic death associated with these organizations have introduced to a whole generation the notion that calm, dispassionate and logical discussion of collective death is a social entertainment.

The methodology commonly involves the concoction of scenarios of action and reaction on the part of deterrer and deterred in a variety of situations—a sort of intellectual ping pong. These exercises are termed "crises games" —simulations of international crises.

Pete Seeger sings:

> Oh, the Rand Corporation is the boon of the world;
> They think all day long for a fee.
> They sit and play games about going up in flames;
> For counters they use you and me, honey bee.
> For counters they use you and me.

Unfortunately, as Chief of Naval Operations Admiral David L. McDonald has testified, human life is not a factor in the mathematical cost-effectiveness equations that are fed into computers because there is no way to assign "intrinsic value" and "finite proportions" to it.

In working out the denouements of these war-peace games, the shapers of strategy have wedded computer techniques to the laws of statistics and probability applicable to the theory of games. It would spoil the fun, at this point, to suggest that the game analogy presupposes rationality and rules while the facts of life pose irrationality. Otherwise, the military intellectuals would have to admit that an irrational world requires the elimination of thermonuclear weapons and, ultimately, disarmament. This they obviously cannot afford to do. Instead, the result has been the creation of a mathematics of death—a calculus of warfare—in which military planning becomes wholly depersonalized and mechanistic.

For a cold-blooded practitioner of nuclear gamesmanship, only one conclusion is possible. Dr. Kahn expresses it in his usual blunt manner: "According to my *morality* the use of nuclear weapons can be justified if the consequences of using them, awful as they are, are better than the consequences of not using them."

The trouble with all these exercises is that human nature—and human folly and human error—is largely unpredictable; and governments, being composed of men and not machines, will not be bound by form charts.

The possibility of failure of the system of deterrence does not daunt our planners. They do not shrink from thinking about the unthinkable. It is reported that our Mr. McNamara can discuss with total impassivity what happens if X planes or missiles drop Y nuclear bombs on Z country. His voice evidently doesn't go up, down, loud or soft, while he tells you that only 125 million or 175 million will be dead in an attack.

After all, it should be clear to the citizen by now that the heart of a credible deterrent in a nuclear age lies in being prepared to face the consequences, should deterrence fail. It follows that if a system to prevent instant war breaks down, instant war is what you get. For we face the fantastic paradox in which the fundamental instruments for preventing war mean that war, if it comes, must be more dreadful than the imagination can conceive.

But, don't worry. Our leaders have even figured out the consequences of a failure of the system of deterrence. Enter the computer and its attendants. We may describe them, with J. B. Priestley, as the "V. I. P. Highest Priority-Top Secret-Top People Class, men now so conditioned by this atmosphere of power politics, intrigue, secrecy, insane invention, that they are more than half barmy."

Drunk with the heady wine of power politics, military strategy, and limitless power of destruction, the brain trust thrusts forward, creating mathematical models of future wars. If the research organizations thought of a nuclear war as the end of history, they would put themselves out of business and seriously curtail the lucrative flow of government contracts. Thus, with a great effort, they force themselves to think of such a war as something to experience, survive, and rebuild from afterward.

Having fought their imaginary war in an imaginary computer world, the university and foundation warriors have concluded that, with sufficient preparation, we actually will be able to survive and recuperate if deterrence fails. Dr. Kahn, for instance, believes that even if the casualties ran to one-quarter or one-half of the population, the survivors would not just lie down and die. Nor would they necessarily suffer a disastrous social disorganization: life would go on and the necessary readjustment would be made. Time will pass and women will again bear children and we will build new armies and new weapons and there will be a new generation of strategists of deterrence.

Dr. Kahn states in his book *On Thermonuclear War,* "Despite a widespread belief to the contrary, objective studies indicate that even though the amount of human tragedy would be greatly increased in the postwar world, the increase would not preclude normal and happy lives for the majority of survivors and their descendants." He is convinced that it should be possible "to restore a reasonable facsimile of the prewar society." No doubt with home freezers, color television, and split level houses with two automobiles parked in their garages.

It should be noted that not all scientists hold this cheerful view. Professor Harrison Brown, for instance, believes that with the "enormous complexity of our interlocking networks of mines, factories and communications . . . the incredible complexity and congestion of a megalopolis . . . not very many H bombs, well placed, would suffice to bring our entire industrial complex to a grinding halt. Recovery from major disruption may literally be impossible because the tools will be too complicated and the necessary raw materials too dispersed." Professor Brown concludes, "I would give further odds that mankind would then be destined to live an agrarian existence for the duration of its lifetime as a species."

Max Born, the German nuclear physicist, predicts that the mother country, after being saved from aggression, will look like a landscape on the moon.

Tom Stonier, the author of the chilling *Nuclear Disaster*, concludes: "A demoralized country neither rebuilds nor recovers rapidly. Instead, social institutions disappear, individual skills are lost, knowledge recedes, and the pall of a dark age descends." This book should make it abundantly clear that the quickest way to remove a country from the mainstream of history is to subject it to thermonuclear attack.

Be that as it may, with an "act of iron will," Dr. Kahn addresses himself to the question of how much tragedy is acceptable and goes about the "task of distinguishing among the possible degrees of awfulness." He comes up with a table of "Tragic but Distinguishable Postwar States:"

Dead (of United States Population)	Years Required for Economic Recuperation
2 million	1 year
5	2
10	5
20	10
40	20
80	50
160	100

His footnote to the table is worth repeating, "Will the survivors envy the dead?"

The key to the probability of survival seems to be the words "with sufficient preparation." An expert like Henry A. Kissinger stresses that "it is important to prepare a familiar environment in advance of the catastrophe of all-out war." This advice has not been ignored by the centers of power nor by the Pentagon's E-ring. Mr. Mc-Namara has declared "Civil defense is an integral and essential part of our overall defense posture."

Civil defense has already opened one underground center at Denton, Texas, and is asking for $7.8 million to start building seven more underground command posts that would be used to direct recovery after an attack on the United States. An Office of Emergency Planning has been set up with a staff of about 310 to see that the country is prepared to recover from the disaster of nuclear war. Presumably, the survivors will emerge as from a Noah's ark to rebuild American life and society.

It would be a pity if a thermonuclear war should break out over the heads of a psychologically unprepared population, because such an eventuality might lead to a loss of faith in society and government. For there is one thing upon which all theorists of deterrence agree and that is that we will still have a country after a nuclear war. Dr. Kahn states, "I further believe that in the pre-1965 period, possibly extending into the late sixties or early seventies, it will indeed be possible (if proper preparations have been made) to still have a country after most wars."

Dr. Edward Teller flatly declares, "We could survive as a nation and the great majority of our citizens can actually survive an atomic attack." He goes on to state optimistically, "We can, after a number of austere but not necessarily terrible years, rebuild our country to its old and to a better strength."

The experts do not tell us whether we ourselves will survive or if we will still have our parents or our wives or our husbands or our children or the rest of our families or friends or neighbors. But we are assured that the nation will survive and that should be a great comfort to us. One is reminded of a Bill Mauldin cartoon showing a battered human emerging from a shattered shelter, crying hysterically, "We won!"

One can imagine our proverbial spy from Mars retreating from this insane planet. He peers down through the familiar mushroom clouds at a United States whose people have been murdered, its cities crumbled, its rivers poisoned, its vegetation defoliated, its food contaminated, its air polluted, its surface crystallized to a greenish glasslike trinitite. But despite the man made tidal waves obliterating its boundaries, he can still discern the outlines of the Atlantic and Pacific Oceans, the Great Lakes, the Gulf of Mexico. Yes, it does our hearts good to know that the nation survives. God bless America.

We have been glibly talking about deterrence as if it were an immutable doctrine, capable of exact definition. On the contrary, the truth is that deterrence is a shifting concept whose meaning shifts from country to country and in each country from time to time. It is most difficult to interpret the semantics of nuclear war-gaming, especially when the allied nations cannot even agree on fundamentals among themselves.

For instance, Secretary of State John Foster Dulles first enunciated the policy of "massive retaliation" in 1954; under this system instant, massive nuclear retaliation would be unleashed in a counter-city strategy as the answer to all shapes of military and political aggression. The reply would be a spasm response—all out retaliation with everything we have.

The theory behind this was that if it were made obvious that even small, non-nuclear aggression would be met with the full force of atomic weapons, then such aggressions would not occur. Mr. Dulles' plan might be retitled, "Or how to turn little wars into big wars." Limited aggression did occur and President Eisenhower could not bring himself to follow through with the threat proclaimed by his Administration. The President found that every pinprick of provocation could not be met with a nuclear war. In other words, neither the enemy nor the American government believed in the credibility of the deterrent. The tough shibboleths were found empty and wanting.

Thus, in the abovementioned speech at the University of Michigan in June 1962, Secretary of Defense Robert

S. McNamara outlined a new no-city strategy. In order to give the enemy "the strongest imaginable incentive to refrain from striking our cities," he said, "the United States has come to the conclusion, that to the extent possible, basic military strategy in a possible general war should be approached in much the same way that more conventional military operations have been regarded in the past. That is to say, principal military objectives . . . should be the destruction of the enemy's military forces, not of his civilian population." This is the so-called counterforce concept.

This strategy is based on the probability that no first strike will ever destroy all the missiles. Then, in retaliation, all ruin will rain on the attacker's cities. An incentive is thus offered to refrain from striking the cities in the first strike. Theoretically, sufficient power is kept on reserve to accomplish this objective on a second strike, if necessary. With no advantage to be gained by striking first and no disadvantage to be suffered by striking second, there will be no motive for either surprise or preemptive attack.

Chairman Khrushchev characterized Mr. McNamara's speech as a "monstrous proposal" that sought "to legalize nuclear war and thereby the murder of millions upon millions of people." He rightly declared that "nuclear missile war erases the line between the battlefield and the rear" and that "it is the civilian population that will be the first prey of the weapons of mass annihilation." Since a substantial portion of the Soviet rocket force is largely unprotected, the Russians might be tempted in some future showdown, to fire their vulnerable missiles rather than take the chance of their being destroyed on their launching pads.

Professor Henry A. Kissenger raises similar objections

to the counter-force theory as "not in accord with the realities of the strategic equation. For a war of attrition . . . cannot be in the interest of the weaker side. Against a numerically superior opponent, the sensible strategy would be to shock him into stopping his attack while some forces remain, by attacking objectives of great value to him—such as cities."

Secretary McNamara seemed to have had second thoughts. He began to find it unlikely that an enemy would refrain from attacking American cities, since studies and re-studies have demonstrated the virtual impossibility of separating military from non-military targets in a general nuclear war. Besides, he began to realize that a counterforce strategy could have very little meaning in a missile age where retaliatory strikes would arrive only to find that most of the enemy missiles had been fired in the first strike and the rest had been hidden or protected.

So, *circa* 1964, the Secretary seemed to veer to a new damage-limiting strategy—a flexible or graduated deterrence, a strategy of choice, or as Hanson W. Baldwin puts it in lay language, "to make the punishment fit the crime." Fortuitously, such a policy requires a considerably larger force and that much greater expenditure on armaments, thus showering more of the benefits of deterrence upon workers, businessmen, generals and statesmen. Here is something for everybody.

More important, the benefits of graduated deterrence are showered upon the different Services—the Army, the Navy, and the Air Force. Each is waging a fierce struggle for dominance; tugging and pulling for the hog size share of jobs, personnel, money, prestige, weapon systems and, incidentally, power.

The explanation for flexible deterrence—like Mr. Baldwin's—sounds as glib as the libretto for a Gilbert and Sullivan operetta. Actually, the doctrine is sheer Madison Avenue, a selling job marketed to the public by captive research organizations. Here is the way the whole business of concocting a particular theory of deterrence works.

First, a private industrial complex develops a set of weapons which it wishes to sell to a particular Service. The Service is impressed by the line and expresses an interest in buying. At this point, the task falls upon the brain trust to formulate an elaborate rationalization after the fact—in which these weapons are the key element.

Now, the organized and powerful pressure lobbies, in and outside Congress, of each Service move in for the hard sell. The result is the Mix, where the quiver of each branch bristles with the widest array of armaments, from conventional to thermonuclear. Here is another case of achieving the best of all possible worlds for all concerned. The strategy of choice is the perfect answer, not to meet the needs of the people for security, but to placate the insatiable demands of the Services for more and more power.

It is the opinion of Arthur I. Waskow that, because the Mix provides all branches of the armed services with all sorts of weapons, confusion would be greatly increased in case thermonuclear war were to come. Mr. Waskow believes that such a confounding of strategies "would be an unexampled catastrophe all around the globe."

The prewar rivalries of Polaris captains, Titan generals and SAC commanders would be forced, during the war itself, into a fantastic competition of attack. They would all be fighting, not from any clear strategy of what targets to hit, but from a deliberate helter-skelter of intentions. Without any clear directions as to when, where and why to fire, components of the Mix would soon be firing at everything in sight. As political control broke down and communications disintegrated in the midst of the fighting, the Mix might well spawn a warlord atmosphere. Each possessor of nuclear weapons would become a law unto himself. The gentle reader will recall with a chill the movie *Bedford Incident*, starring Richard Widmark.

This possibility is not far-fetched, because Atomic War I will undoubtedly begin with the firing of missiles directly overhead into space. Their nuclear warheads, triggered to go off at a high altitude, would create an immense auroral display, like an intense solar flare or magnetic storm, jamming the Ballistic Missile Early Warning System (BMEWS) and blacking out radio communication and satellite detection systems. Liddell Hart, the eminent military authority, for instance, threw up his hands at any attempt to predict the course of a thermonuclear war. He wrote, "There is no sense even in planning for such a war. The destruction and chaos would be so great within a few hours that the war could not continue in any organized sense."

But the final curtain has not yet fallen on the drama of deterrence. Obviously, the doctrine of flexible deterrence costs lots of money. As the countries of both East and West begin to feel the monetary pinch of sagging economies, the tendency is to go back to the earlier doctrine of "a bigger bang for a buck." Strangely enough, while this shift is taking place, the defense ministers of NATO, meeting for the first time without France on May 9, 1967, formally scrapped the ten-year-old concept of massive retaliation and adopted the strategy of flexible response as the official doctrine of the alliance.

Despite the method of deterrence chosen, Mr. McNamara leaves us with one consoling thought, stressing that the United States still possessed "a clear and unmistakable ability to destroy an aggressor as a viable society, even after our forces have been attacked." In other words, we shall contain the enemy—dead or alive.

Everyone knows that France sets the style and does not follow. So General De Gaulle and his country cling to the old discarded all azimuths massive retaliation doctrine. Only they call it "force de frappe." French military policy still calls for immediate nuclear war in any conflict in which it is involved. Without coordination of strategic doctrines between the two estranged allies, what happens when le grand Charles pushes the button and blows up selected Russian cities before Uncle Sam is ready? This French attitude nullifies the entire American strategy. All the billions spent on graduated deterrence go down the drain at the whim of France because the Russians certainly are not going to differentiate from which Western point the bombs originated.

What are the British doing with their miniscule atomic arsenal? They claim that without it, they would be exposed to nuclear blackmail. One suspects that it is the final clutching at the grandeur and prestige that once belonged to this sceptred isle.

Now that Russia is deploying a new missile defense system around the Soviet Union, the value of the few offensive nuclear missiles planned by France and Britain would be neutralized. Only the American strategic force, with its large number of missiles containing advanced penetration devices, would have any chance of piercing such a defense.

Bernard Baruch, in his famous introductory remarks of June 14, 1946, to the United Nations Atomic Energy Commission, declared, "We are here to make a choice between the quick and the dead. That is our business. . . . If we fail, then we have damned every man to be the slave of Fear. Let us not deceive ourselves. We must elect World Peace or World Destruction." The truth is that deterrence has damned every man to be the slave of Fear.

President Johnson recognizes that the "fearsome engines" of today are not mere symptoms of intention. "Weapons have themselves become a cause of fear and a cause of distrust among other nations. As weapons become more numerous and more deadly, fear and tension grow." Distrust, fear, and tension—these are the products of deterrence and one does not need the authority of a psychologist with the eminence of Erich Fromm to know that these are also the causes of war. A statement made by eighteen Nobel Prize winners, on July 15, 1955, states, "We think it is a delusion if governments believe they can avoid war for a long time through fear of these weapons. Fear and tension have often engendered wars." One of the greatest dangers posed by all these experts and all these theories is the impression that avoidance of a nuclear war is simply a matter of skillful crisis management.

Must we not ask, with George F. Kennan, "What sort of a life is it to which these devotees of the weapons race would see us condemned?" Would we be sacrificing all the values which make it worthwhile to live well at all?

Must we come to the somber conclusion that we would not be able to maintain a favorable position in this race without giving up our way of life—freedom and democracy—as rapidly as possible? Dr. Kahn states, "We must admit that this freedom will be lost, whether the deterrent works or does not work."

In the effort to conduct international relations primarily by military methods in accordance with the dictates of the doctrine of deterrence, we have been defeating ourselves internally. The methods of the arms race are inconsistent with the goals of freedom in society, with the value of human life, with the dignity of the individual. Norman Thomas has noted that military conscription is in "complete contravention of any true notion of individual freedom" and the "chief denial of civil liberty of which the state is capable."

The organs of democratic society have been enfeebled by the hobbling of the individual citizen, official classified secrecy, repression, suspicion, conformism, and the corruption of absolute power shielded from public criticism.

"We must anticipate," with United States Air Force Chief of Staff General John Paul McConnell, "that the impact of our military establishment on every phase of our national effort and every facet of our society will become even greater and more profound than it is today."

Perhaps security based on the nuclear deterrent is only a fool's paradise. Certainly, it did not prevent dangerous adventures in Berlin, Greece, Turkey, Iran, Formosa, Korea, Lebanon, Cuba, Laos, Vietnam, and elsewhere. Does deterrence, then, prevent wars or does it make wars possible by massing the weapons of wholesale destruction?

One is drawn to the conclusion that the theory of deterrence is a deterrent not to war, but to peace—a deterrent to constructive, realistic peace negotiation. The term deterrence becomes another euphemism for the arms race—a blueprint for winning the next war.

One is forced to wonder whether our military, public and industrial leaders who guide the destinies of the theory of deterrence are really the guardians of our safety, as we have imagined. Perhaps they are the exact reverse —the greatest menace to our safety. Must we not conclude that a deterrent which can never be used without destroying both deterrer and deterred is not a deterrent but a constant threat?

The basic difficulty is that our leaders have not yet disabused themselves of the Great Illusion that there can be a victor in atomic war. Norman Angell demonstrated in his 1910 book, *Great Illusion*, that war is economically unprofitable with respect to trade and markets. Now the costs of thermonuclear war have become so great that both the victor and the vanquished will be utterly and absolutely defeated in terms of lives, trade, markets, territory —everything.

Secretary of State Dean Rusk has said, "Winning is a very risky phrase. We're in a nuclear period and the survival of the human race is at stake. These events can get out of control unless we're very careful." Unfortunately, the actions of Mr. Rusk and of the United States government too often belie these sentiments.

The entire doctrine of deterrence distills down to the summary offered by Giuló Douhet, one of the early prophets of the theory: "We must, therefore, resign ourselves to the offensives the enemy inflicts upon us, while striving to put all our resources to work to inflict even heavier ones upon him."

The citizen may well ask whether we have here crossed the nonsense line and whether massive deterrence is not massive nonsense. In the words of Amitai Etzione, "Tin will turn to gold and vodka to whiskey before there will be safety in piles of guns and nuclear explosives."

Mankind is trapped in the absurd position of arming in order to disarm, of squandering billions of dollars on horrifying weapons which are only to be used as toys (or bribes) by millions of grown, drafted soldiers, of assigning thousands of military specialists to draw up plans of war operations which are to be used only as ticker tape. What lunatic logic induces us to even consider all out nuclear war in defense of Western civilization when we must know that our civilization could not possibly survive such a catastrophe? How many times do we have to relearn the lesson that to fight a war to end the danger of war is an absurdity?

Yet, believe it or not, the posture of deterrence which we have described in this chapter is the official position of the governments of the United States, the Soviet Union, Red China, France, and of almost every other major country on earth. Doesn't the fact that this policy is adhered to almost universally mean that it is almost God ordained and right? Not necessarily. Slavery, feudalism, absolute monarchy, belief in witches, burning at the stake for heresy, ideas that the earth was flat or that the sun revolved about it, cottage industries—all these concepts hung on for endless ages after these practices and beliefs had completely outgrown their usefulness.

Walter Millis and other peddlers of soporific pills would

lull us to sleep with the argument that so long as the system of deterrence has kept us alive since 1945, why shouldn't the system continue to work its magic spell indefinitely.

Mr. Millis deserves to be quoted verbatim. He writes, "The great nuclear weapons appear to have introduced whatever measure of military stability exists in the present world. Clearly, it is a present stability purchased only at the price of a frightful future risk; but it seems to be the great weapons, more than any other factor, that we owe the fact that we are not now tearing ourselves to pieces in a third global war. Can we, then, contemplate a policy which would not begin by trying simply to abolish them, but rather by trying consciously to balance them, to conserve the stabilities which they do provide while reducing or eliminating the appalling instabilities implicit in their competitive technical development."

Apologists like Mr. Millis would have us believe that the monstrous balance of terror is really a "balance of prudence." Greater mayhem has not been committed against the English language since hydrogen bombs were termed "clean."

It is eerie how ancient and discarded historical theories crop up again and again. Before 1914 and 1939 and other wars, it was the balance of power theory which was credited with preserving the peace. Lowes Dickinson rightly observed then that the balance of power theory professed balance but pursued imbalance, that, "It is thus, in fact, a perpetual effort to get the better of the balance, and as this effort is prosecuted on both sides, the ultimate issue is war." In the lament of the great Baroness von Suttner,

"O, this balance of power! what blood-thirsty diplomatic hypocrite invented this hollow phrase?"

The H bomb has become the Holy Grail of our age, the magic deterrent which will hypnotize the guns and neutralize the enemy. Bow down and worship this all-powerful H idol. A more grotesque program of disarmament cannot be imagined. H bombs can only be provocative; they can never be forces for stability. Dr. Ralph E. Lapp declares, "We must recognize that the peace of nuclear terror cannot endure for long."

Love that bomb, embrace it, hug the monster to your breast. Ignore the warning of Herman Kahn that the probability of war occurring becomes very high when the "game of chicken" is played once too often.

It is submitted that the fact that a general nuclear war is not raging today proves absolutely nothing. Before 1914 and 1939, many great theorists established beyond cavil that wars were obsolete. It was George Santayana who warned that, "Those who cannot remember the past are condemned to repeat it." Mr. Millis's predictions of things to come proved erroneous in the cases of Vietnam and the Dominican Republic. Perhaps, he might also be proven wrong with respect to the possibility of the failure of deterrence. Then what remedy does mankind have against these sandmen? One is reminded of the fallout shelter manufacturer who offered double your money back if his product did not prove satisfactory.

Yet, in the main, the worker, the businessman, the statesman, even the soldier, are not evil men. It is inconceivable that the workingman, for the sake of a job and a few hours of overtime; the businessman, for the sake of thirty pieces of silver; the statesman, for the sake of basking a few fleeting moments in the spotlight of power;

> (My Name is Ozymandias, king of kings:
> Look on my works, ye Mighty and despair!
> Nothing beside remains. Round the decay
> Of that colossal wreck, boundless and bare,
> The lone and level sands stretch far away.)

the general, for the sake of a handful of tawdry medals and faded ribbons, would gravely risk their own lives, the lives of their loved ones, and the lives of their children's children for all time.

It must be that these worthy people are so wrapped up in the daily necessities and trivialities that they do not look beyond the tips of their noses. What does it avail us if we gain today but lose tomorrow and all tomorrows. It is up to the citizen to lift up his eyes and squarely face the facts and implications of the theory of deterrence.

All our experience of two centuries reminds us that to be prepared for war is one of the most effectual means of getting war. The citizen must then see the disquieting similarities to the pre-1914 and pre-1939 eras. He must see that reliance on the great deterrent is wishful thinking —a great myth and a great fiction. In the light of history, faith in the deterrent can best be considered mystical. From all human experience, we have no reason to believe that the balance of terror will last. To quote Pope Paul VI, reliance upon the nuclear balance of terror is "an illusory concept."

To die in the pursuit of this illusory concept, this appalling idiocy, would mean that we shall not have died for liberty or freedom, for our country, for our children. We

shall have died for silliness, for absurdity—as tragic actors
in a planetary farce. To entrust the fate of the human race
to this flimsy military theory of deterrence borders on
lunacy. One fears the prophecy of Euripides, "Whom the
Gods would destroy they first make mad." After studying
the doctrine of deterrence, there is only one possible
comment that the citizen can make:

GENTLEMEN, YOU ARE MAD.

If you desire peace, prepare for war; if you would be
chaste, fornicate; if you would be sober, drink; if you
would be thrifty, splurge; if you would love, hate . . .
hate; if you would live, kill . . . kill . . . kill . . . kill . . .

5

Oops, the Bomb Slipped

Indeed, our military and political leaders are themselves skeptical of the ability of deterrence to stave off Atomic War I.

General Omar Bradley said, "We are now speeding inexorably toward a day when even the ingenuity of our scientists may be unable to save us from the consequences of a single rash act or a lone reckless hand upon the switch of an uninterceptable missile . . . Have we already gone too far in this search for peace through the accumulation of peril . . . must we push on to new devices until we inevitably come to judgment before the atom?"

President Kennedy stressed to the United Nations General Assembly, on September 20, 1963, that, "We must continue to seek agreement on measures which prevent war by accident or miscalculation." President Johnson has warned of the danger of "an unintended nuclear exchange." On January 18, 1964, he wrote to Chairman Khrushchev urging "new proposals . . . to reduce the risk of war by accident or design." The Chief Executive followed through three days later with a message to the disarmament conferences in Geneva, proposing, "we must further reduce the danger of war by accident, miscalculation or surprise attack."

Soviet Foreign Minister Andrei A. Gromyko told a news conference, on April 18, 1958, that, "The world is finding itself in a position where atomic war can result from a slightest mistake on the part of an American technician, from carelessness, miscalculation or faulty conclusions on the part of some American officer." Mr. Gromyko might have bracketed a Russian technician or a Russian officer in his warning.

The often quoted Mr. McNamara admonished the Committee on Armed Services of the House of Representatives in 1963: "As the arms race continues, the weapons multiply and become more swift and deadly, the possibility of a global catastrophe, either by miscalculation or design, becomes ever more real." He has also stated, "Proliferation of nuclear weapons capability would increase the likelihood of accidental detonation of a nuclear weapon." British Defense Secretary Denis Healey feels that "an accidental attack or war by mistake is the only real problem faced in Europe."

Sir Michael Wright, who served for thirty-seven years in the British Foreign Service and had been Ambassador to Norway and Iraq as well as a delegate to the Nuclear Tests Conference in 1959-1961, the Ten Nation Disarmament Conference in 1961, and the Eighteen Nation Disarmament Conference in 1962-1963—besides being an adviser in disarmament to the British United Nations delegation in 1961-1962—writes, "To rely for peace upon the indefinite duration of a balance of nuclear forces and upon the self-restraint of a growing number of nuclear powers is an exercise in dangerous living comparable to building a permanent home on the slopes of Mount Etna."

Our political leaders say that a nuclear war by accident or design is possible. Our scientific leaders agree.

We have already quoted Baron Snow to the effect that it is a statistical certainty that some of these fearful weapons "are going to blow up." Lord Charles told the American Association for the Advancement of Science, on December 27, 1960, "within at the most ten years, some of these bombs are going off." He went on, "I am saying this as responsibly as I can. That is the certainty—a certainty of disaster." In the same vein, Professor Amitai Etzione declared, "It can be stated, without reservation, that the longer we live in the shadow of the bombs, the more likely a nuclear war becomes."

Dr. Kahn agrees that, "In a multi-weaponed world, the actual problems and choices are likely to involve accident, miscalculation, blackmail or the irresponsible use of weapons." John B. Witchell, an engineer who resigned from the Canadian Atomic Research Board in protest against nuclear armament, declared, "The demand for instantaneous retaliation leads to a hair-trigger situation which renders nuclear war a statistical certainty."

Dr. Linus Pauling stresses the "present great danger of outbreak of war through some technological or psychological accident." Dr. Leo Szilard rated the chances of avoiding atomic war at between 5 per cent and 10 per cent.

In an article entitled *Accidental War: Some Dangers in the 1960's,* John V. Phelps writes that chances are one in one hundred that a United States nuclear weapon will

explode some time during the next ten years merely because of essentially mechanical malfunctions. How much
do the chances increase if we consider the nuclear weapons of other countries and the possibilities of human
malfunctions? Must we conclude with the great thinker
and philosopher Karl Jaspers that human survival is intel-
lectually improbable? Or as Dr. Reinhold Niebuhr put it,
"war by miscalculation or misadventure is more and more
a probability rather than a possibility."

Perhaps then it is with every justification that Eugene
Burdick and Harvey Wheeler begin their novel *Fail Safe*
as follows: "There is substantial agreement among experts
that an accidental war is possible and that its probability
increases with the increasing complexity of the man machine components which make up our defense system.
This is unfortunately, a 'true' story. The accident may not
occur in the way we describe, but the laws of probability
assure us that ultimately it will occur." Clifton Fadiman's
comment was, "They are not writing fantasy."

Further, our leaders evidently mistrust the posture of
deterrence, for how else can one explain the elaborate fail
safe and permissive action link procedures which have
been instituted. A wide array of administrative and physical restraints have been designed to prevent nuclear firing
in violation of authority. These precautions have gone as
far as the building of barriers on runways used by nuclear-
arms-bearing aircraft to prevent unauthorized takeoffs.

The United States Strategic Air Command has always
maintained rigidly enforced systems of fail safe procedures whereby nuclear armed bombers are at all times
under positive control through the use of a communications system comprising about 1,000 radio and wire cir-

cuits covering more than one million miles. SAC command posts are in constant contact with their aircraft in flight so that the release of their nuclear bombloads will not occur unless an affirmative signal in code is received from higher authority. A malfunction is designed to cause the system to fail safe, not unsafe.

It takes a specific arming action to make an airborne nuclear bomb operational. The crew of a loaded plane could not let it loose until it received specific arming instructions by voice and electronic signal in a controlled and ever-changing pattern.

With the shift away from bomber aircraft toward intercontinental missiles, the emphasis has been on permissive action links. These electromechanical locks, which must be opened by a secret combination before action is possible, have been placed on many weapons since 1961. The arming switch can be tampered with only by disassembling—and therefore by disarming—the weapon. It can be activated only by remote control or by the insertion of a key.

Now an ICBM like the Minuteman is a last-resort weapon; it cannot fail safe. A launch control center, buried 60 feet underground, controls the flight of ten Minuteman missiles with nuclear warheads. A double strongbox within each capsule holds the secret firing orders. Only one man knows the combination to the padlock while the lock inside can be opened only by the second man.

With receipt of the red phone message from SAC headquarters—signaled by a high, warbled, whippoorwill tone —the arming switches would be flipped and the keys inserted in the launch control panel. The missile cannot be launched without a corroborating signal—called a second note—by another launch control center. Once two separate capsules give "go" signals, the irreversible countdown begins. It would last only thirty seconds. The eighty-six-ton lids would be blown away at each silo and an electric spark would ignite the 44,000 pounds of solid fuel in the first stage. The missile would cook in its hole for a second or two and then vault toward the sky. The Minuteman would be irretrievably gone; there is no way to change its course or destroy it from the ground or divert it from an enemy target. A missile must be launched within the relatively brief tactical time available before the attacker strikes home. Otherwise, the missile risks destruction on the ground. Our Mr. McNamara commented, "I need not elaborate on the dangers of this situation."

To command and control the thousands of strategic and tactical warheads stockpiled in hundreds of overseas land bases and aboard ships overseas—many of them in the hands of relatively junior officers—reliance is placed on a most complex communications network. The National Military Command System handles the transmission of over 110 million military messages a year from the outposts of the world over a network of 19 million channel miles. An intricate system of duplicate channels feeding into a central command post in Washington and alternate and emergency command posts elsewhere permit instantaneous communication with any point.

Throughout, control is exercised by a "key" system which extends in an elaborate sequence from the weapons in the field to the command authorities headed by the President. It is combined with a procedural formula that requires at least two men to be present at every level of operation or handling of nuclear weapons. The two-man rule provides that when a weapon is in storage at least two men must stand guard. If a message is received to load the weapon on a plane or mount it on the ground, at least two men must verify the authenticity of the command. To arm or fuse the bomb, at least two men must perform independent, coordinate action.

Even then, the final order to fire the weapon—whether from an airplane, a ground silo or at sea—may depend upon an enabling action controlled by a key in the hands of a man many miles away, who in turn is dependent upon still more distant orders. Two or more men must independently decide the order has been given and they must independently take action. This rule of redundancy, or deliberate duplication, is the prevailing practice.

Aware that 43 per cent of all American armed forces and 40 per cent of all RAF discharges in World War II were for neuropsychiatric causes, the United States Defense Department has adopted regulations requiring the strict screening of military personnel assigned to the control and handling of nuclear devices. A determination is required from the commanding officer that the individual concerned possesses the necessary mental and emotional stability to be trusted with access to the nuclear weapon. Under a human responsibility program, periodic physical and psychological examinations follow to discover and weed out those of its personnel whose emotional instability might lead them to press the fatal button without authorization.

It is uncertain whether similar regulations exist to test the mental balance of the scientists engaged in the war program. Witness the nuclear physicist who went berserk at the Brookhaven National Laboratory in January 1966 and shot three co-workers before committing suicide.

Professor Seymour Melman cites the conclusion of a study of accidental war possibilities by a group of psychiatrists that "No existing tests will reliably screen out individuals susceptible to mental breakdowns. The range of potentially serious psychological problems is extremely wide. The possibly harmful effects of great responsibility, maintained over long time periods in . . . a cold war time role are nearly impossible to predict." And Amitai Etzioni reminds us that "The not infrequent defection of persons painstakingly selected to handle top-secret information shows the inadequacy of all known screening methods."

There is even a remote possibility that a commanding officer may be suffering from a psychopathic or messianic mania. A nut like Captain Queeg is sufficient menace. But what happens when a general is obsessed with the notion that his civilian government is composed of a group of sinister men involved in an "international conspiracy of debauchery and atheistic treachery" to sell out his country? What happens when this general fervently believes that "The oath of office (of a soldier) is an individual covenant with Almighty God from which no man can be released by unconstitutional actions, orders or decisions"?

Believe it or not, we have been quoting from the public statements of General Edwin A. Walker, who commanded the 13,000 troops of the United States 24th Infantry Division in Germany from 1959-1963. It was General Walker who introduced the famous "pro-blue" ideological training program. Note: the 24th Infantry is equipped with nuclear tactical weapons.

General Walker was only taking his cue from his great precursor on horseback, General Douglas MacArthur, who, when he was relieved of his command by President Truman, declared it was "a new and hitherto unknown and dangerous concept that the members of our armed forces owe primary allegiance or loyalty to those who *temporarily* exercise the authority of the Executive Branch of the Government rather than to the country and to the Constitution which they are sworn to defend. No proposition could be more dangerous." Read the military literature. It bristles with references to the civilian heads of state as "gravediggers" who are betraying the nation to an international conspiracy.

What happens when an entire nation, fully armed, goes berserk and suffers a nervous breakdown? Hitler's Germany, Stalin's Russia, and Mussolini's Italy gave that answer.

Another indication of the official mistrust of the command and control system is the hot line, a wire cable connecting the Pentagon in Washington with the Kremlin in Moscow (via London, Copenhagen, Stockholm and Helsinki with an alternate short-wave radio connection via Tangier). If, despite all the precautions, something goes awry perhaps Washington can assure Moscow (or vice versa) that it is all a big mistake—perhaps.

Our leaders would have us believe that the command and control system is so tightly drawn that the final decision—the only decision—to loose atomic war is vested in but one man: the President of the United States. President Johnson has assured us that he has a steady thumb and that "The American people can rest assured we have taken every step man can devise to insure that neither a madman nor a malfunction could trigger nuclear war."

It has probably occurred to the reader that the President would have to be a two-headed wonder with the mind of a computer to receive, sift, weigh and evaluate the millions of bits of often ambiguous information that pour into Washington each day. And then he is expected to make the right decision in micro-seconds—split-seconds belong to an earlier, slower moving age—because if he hesitated any longer it would be too late. There are just too many uncertainties and too many choices. Perhaps personal Presidential control over atomic war is so much more technological nonsense, another pretense, another myth of our age.

For example, President Truman admitted that so much was happening so fast on so many fronts in February and March 1945 that he despaired of keeping up with the rush of events.

There is just too little time and too many missiles, too many buttons, too many people with potential decision power, too many weapons, too many reports, too many risks, too many tensions, too many crises in too many far flung places. The information that reaches the President is distilled by his subordinates from information that has been distilled by their subordinates from information that . . . . Considering the huge sums spent on the Central Intelligence Agency and the several service intelligence units, how was it possible to distill such faulty information to the highest executives in connection with the Bay of Pigs fiasco and the Vietnam cul-de-sac?

The officials at the top are completely dependent for information on their underlings and there is no way for these decision-making officials to get this information if their subordinates do not think it is important. First, there is a marked tendency among subordinates everywhere to tell their superiors what they think their superiors wish to hear. Second, facts must be interpreted and if the interpreter is overcredulous, or oversanguine, or overpugnacious, or oversuspicious, or—worst of all—the victim of some fixation as to what the facts must mean, he can give a fatal slant to the best-informed State Department.

For instance, take the American intervention in the Dominican Republic in April 1965. Senator J. W. Fulbright, Chairman of the Senate Foreign Relations Committee, after a "painstaking review," concluded, "The principal reason for the failure of the American policy in Santo Domingo was faulty advice given to the President by his representatives in the Dominican Republic at the time of acute crisis. Much of this advice was based on misjudgment of the facts of the situation; some of it appears to have been based on inadequate evidence or, in some cases, simply false information. On the basis of the information and counsel he received, the President [Johnson] could hardly have acted other than he did; it is very difficult to understand, however, why so much unsound advice was given him."

Nor does it follow that executive orders are always scrupulously and promptly carried out. Months before the Cuban crisis, President Kennedy ordered that the American missile bases in Turkey be shut down. Twice he ordered it; twice he was ignored. Mr. Kennedy explained, "There's always some so-and-so who doesn't get the word."

The citizen can be assured that, at that awful, terrible moment, the same chaos will prevail as at Pearl Harbor; or as at Dallas, when President Kennedy was assassinated; or as at Moscow, on June 22, 1941, when the Nazis invaded the Soviet Union and a panicky Stalin (as recounted

by Ivan M. Maisky) locked himself in his study and refused to give orders; or as at every other crucial moment
in history. At the moment of truth, some unknown, un-
ranked soldier will undoubtedly give the signal for Armageddon. The way in which a particular convoy to Berlin
is stopped will determine the response much more than
any preconceived Presidential plan.

The beginning of wisdom in the discussion of accidental war is the realization that no system devised by
man can ever be mechanically and emotionally foolproof.
Even with the most careful mutual and unilateral arrangements, the possibility of accidents or errors at any time,
anywhere—caused by a relatively minor functionary setting off a disastrous chain of events—will exist. How
many villages like Beduc and Locthuonghiet have been
bombed in error?

If there is any thing that is certain in this world it is
that accidents will happen. No machine is perfect. No
human being is free from error. It is common sense that
the more weapons, automation, and complexity of control
mechanisms there are, the more proneness to accident
exists. Even a most unlikely event could possibly happen
if the right conditions for it persisted long enough. The
consequences of a mistake, of an error of judgment, will
become incalculable. The "impossible" malfunction of the
foolproof power system in Northeastern United States,
on November 9, 1965, is an example of the frightening
possibilities. The Mending Apparatus may not function.
An United States 1952 "Progress Report on Reliability of
Electronic Equipment" found only 33 per cent of Navy
equipment operating satisfactorily. Murphy's law, "whatever can go wrong will go wrong," will continue to prevail.

The peoples of the world must forever after stand hostage to a deviant, fanatical, aberrant or psychotic personality; a false alarm, an errant meteor, a mistaken judgment, someone's unauthorized or irresponsible behavior, an act of sabotage, an equipment failure, a stuck button, or a loose screw or bolt. As the Rev. Michael Scott and Bertrand Russell put it in their manifesto, "Act or Perish" in October 1960: "Every day and at every moment of every day, a trivial accident, a failure to distinguish a meteor from a bomber, or a fit of temporary insanity in one single man may cause a nuclear world war, which, in all likelihood, will put an end to man and to all higher forms of animal life."

The citizen can also be assured that the inevitable miscalculation will come along sooner or later. If we are lucky, perhaps we will get by for a while with only an occasional city or town destroyed every now and then as a result of accident, unauthorized behavior or blackmail. The possibilities of accident will increase, of course, as smaller, or less stable, governments attain nuclear capability. Mankind is doomed to walk gingerly forever after on atomic eggs.

It is not possible to create such an overwhelming, nuclear technology, and to place in command of it men so superbly conditioned to fire it, without realizing the objective of the entire effort. Anyone who continually keeps his finger on the button, in a continual state of hair-trigger alert, takes the risk of firing by accident. And there have been any number of accidental near disasters in which the Strategic Air Command has reached fail safe. (One often wonders as to what will happen when the United States and the Soviet Union both reach fail safe at the same time.)

For instance, in July 1965 two American marines climbed into a B-57 jet at the Danang base in South Vietnam and threatened to take off and bomb Hanoi. In 1958 a special weapons maintenance sergeant went berserk and threatened to fire a pistol at a nuclear bomb.

Despite the most rigid secrecy that shrouds incidents of this type, it is known that United States forces have been involved in at least fifty accidents concerning nuclear weapons. One of these occurred in North Africa, one in England and three others in other foreign countries. In one case, where an Air Force B52 bomber crashed near Eureka, North Carolina, in June 1961, the nuclear weapon was found with four of its five interlocking safety catches sprung. In 1956, a B-36 bomber dropped an atomic bomb on barren territory near Kirkland Air Force Base, New Mexico. In 1958, a bomber jettisoned an atomic bomb off the Georgia coast. In January, 1967 a runaway Mace test missile veered over Cuba. Several months later a 10,000 pound Army Pershing missile, fired from Utah, went off course and landed in Mexico.

On another occasion, in January, 1966, a thousand Spanish and American soldiers, with geiger counters, beat through the vegetable patches around Palomares in search of four hydrogen bombs of twenty-five megatons each which were lost when two American planes collided over Spain. The hazards of the nuclear age were brought home to these insular farmers, when 1,500 tons of radioactive earth and vegetation had to be scraped up and shipped to the United States. The maximum amount of the Plutonium spilled that can be taken safely inside the human body is about the size of a speck of dust.

Two years later, another B-52 bomber, carrying the same number of H bombs, crashed into the ice off Greenland. Following this crash, the Soviet Union protested continuance of nuclear-armed airborne alert flights by B-52's, contending that such flights were "senseless" from a military standpoint in view of the development of nuclear missiles. After first claiming that "world tensions make necessary the carrying out of such flights in the interests of collective security against the threat posed by Soviet nuclear forces," the United States saw the logic of the situation and suspended further flights.

On October 5, 1960, the Ballistics Missiles Early Warning System of the North American Defense Command Headquarters at Colorado Springs flashed the alarm of an attack from the Soviet Union. Only the fact that an officer remembered that Chairman Khrushchev was then in the United States prevented a major confrontation. Actually, the Thule, Greenland, station had misidentified radar signals bouncing off the moon as long-range missiles launched against North America. On another occasion, there was a false radar alarm that a Soviet air armada was moving against Turkey. Bertrand Russell has warned that "radar technology is such that a slight technical failure or the appearance of a natural phenomenon can trigger a nuclear war." What would happen if a large meteor, similar to the ones which struck Siberia in 1908 and Vladivostok in 1947, should appear on a radar screen?

As we have mentioned, so toxic is Plutonium 238 that the maximum permissible burden of the material in the bodies of atomic workers has been set at the speck like amount of two-billionths of a gram. Yet 2.2 pounds of this material disappeared over the east coast of Africa, in April, 1964, because someone forgot to throw a switch.

Only God knows how many nuclear near-misses were

experienced by the Russians, the English, the French and the Chinese.

It would appear that as long as the nuclear deterrent system continues as the basis for maintaining security, peace will remain an utterly perilous and artificial thing that man simply does not have the capacity to manage.

It would further seem that the human race has become the very sorry thing that General Eisenhower predicted because man's intelligence cannot control the great weapons that he has produced. The weapons which we have created have turned against us; they have taken over and are deciding our fates. These lethal devices have developed into an objective power over us, growing out of our control, thwarting our calculations. As Sir Winston Churchill said, "As the ill-fated nations approached the verge, the sinister machines of war began to develop their own momentum and even to take control themselves."

What is so dangerous here is that a single inadvertent mistake, made by only one of millions of Americans, Russians, English, French or Chinese—one lost nerve or one lost head—could set fire to the entire world. Thus, a billion or more lives hang in the balance and mankind holds its breath every time there is an interbloc confrontation on the Berlin-Helmstedt autobahn, at the Berlin wall, in the Sea of Japan, in Haiphong harbor, along the Chinese border, or at one of dozens of friction points, where the two camps rub edges with each other. And such a mistake could only be made once—once for all time.

Accidental war can also flower through escalation. Our human IBM machine, former Defense Secretary McNamara talks of a "strategy of controlled response"—of applying United States military power in a selective, measured manner. But is it really possible to limit and contain a conflict within predetermined limits once it has begun? Former Deputy Secretary of Defense Roswell Gilpatric has stated, "I, for one, have never believed in a so-called limited nuclear war. I just don't know how you build a limit into it once you start using any kind of nuclear bang."

Escalation begets escalation. The step from one degree of violence to the next is almost imperceptible and each step appears as an unavoidable consequence of the preceding one. Once taken, it is difficult to retract the step; as John Hersey points out, "The end point of these little steps is horror and oblivion. Wars have a way of getting out of hand." They outrun intentions. The phrase "One damn thing leads to another" is about as accurate a description of the process of escalation as any. It is with good reason, then, that people shudder when shooting is heard anywhere in the world.

It is easy for the side that is winning the battles to prattle about a war limited in scope, involvement and objective. But for any nation there can be no substitute for victory on the battlefield. Experience teaches us that the losing side, in desperation and in mounting ferocity— in the throes of its national agony—will not hesitate to wreak its vengeance on the other side while there is one remaining bomb or warhead in its bins and one last ounce of vehicular strength left in its system to throw it. It is even doubtful whether winning nations, once the threshold of violence has been crossed, will pay attention to the subtle gradations of strategy worked out in the ivory towers of institutes or universities.

This is the sense of the statement released by Moscow, on August 30, 1961, when the Soviets decided to resume nuclear tests: "The experience of history teaches that it has never been possible to keep the fire of war within predetermined limits. Wars have inexorable severe laws of their own. An aggressor starts a war to bring his victim to its knees and to impose his will on it. But even the aggressor is aware that in the case of defeat the fate that he was preparing for his victim will befall him. Therefore, each state that takes part in the war, regardless of the fact whether it attacks or defends, will stop at nothing for attaining victory and will not accept defeat without having used and spent all means in its possession of waging war. Under these conditions any armed conflict, even insignificant at first, would inevitably grow into a universal rocket and nuclear war should the nuclear powers have been drawn into it."

Chairman Khrushchev told Cyrus Sulzberger of the *New York Times* on September 5, 1961, "Let us assume both sides were to promise not to employ nuclear weapons, but retained their stockpiles. What would happen if the imperialists unleashed war? In such a war if any side should feel it was losing, would it not use nuclear weapons to avoid defeat? It would undoubtedly use its nuclear bombs. Furthermore, let me refer to this example; at the close of World War II the United States was considerably stronger than Japan and was waging successful offensive action against it. Yet, to bring victory closer, the United States dropped atomic bombs on Japanese cities. All this goes to show that if atomic weapons are preserved and if war is unleashed it will be a thermonuclear war."

In a similar vein, Lord Tedder, the wartime head of the British Air Force, has stated, "To believe that there will be tactical atomic weapons which could be used without leading to the use of the ultimate so-called strategic weapons would be to live in a fool's paradise."

The situation in Vietnam is a classic example of escalation. On September 2, 1963, President Kennedy said in an interview broadcast the nation wide, "I don't think that unless a greater effort is made by the [South Vietnam] Government to win popular support, that the war can be won out there. In the final analysis, it's their war. They are the ones that have to win it or lose it." Yet, the world has seen how civilian technical assistance and military advisory missions within South Vietnamese territory have insidiously advanced to the point of bombing outside that territory by the United States Air Force and Navy; has seen how a few Air Force instructors grew to giant American air bases, which necessarily required perimeter defense, which inescapably led to ground combat, which inevitably expanded into formal ground warfare; has seen how a handful of consultants begat an invading force of hundreds of thousands of American combatants armed with the latest equipment; has seen how a Vietnamese civil war aided by Americans became an American war fought over the burned villages and the dead bodies of Vietnamese from both South and North. Until the beginning of peace negotiations the Vietnam war daily threatened to spill over the frontiers and involve the entire world. The Duke of Wellington said, "Great powers do not fight small wars."

James Reston, Executive Editor of the *New York Times* reports that President Kennedy intensified the war in Vietnam "not because the situation on the ground demanded it in Vietnam," but because the President "wanted

to prove a diplomatic point, not a military point." Mr.
Kennedy was seeking to demonstrate his credibility and
his manliness to Chairman Khrushchev. Mr. Reston concluded, "That, I think, is where we began to get off the
track."

In other words, the United States is not fighting to save
South Vietnam for the South Vietnamese; the United
States is fighting to save face for the United States. In
this age of deterrence, face, according to Thomas C.
Schelling, is "one of the few things worth fighting over."
Mr. Schelling defines face as "a country's reputation for
action; the expectations other countries have about its
behavior." He believes that "Soviet expectations about
the behavior of the United States are one of the most valuable assets we possess in world affairs," and that the 30,000
dead suffered in Korea for this cause "was undoubtedly
worth it." Is history beginning to repeat itself in Thailand?

Walter Lippmann compares escalation to the gambler
who, having lost one round, doubles his bets in the hope
of recovering what he has lost.

Because the entire concept of war by escalation or miscalculation is so important, and because there are so many
valid analogies between July 1914 and almost any crisis
month of today, it should be interesting to turn to World
War I for a moment. The more historians study the be-
ginnings of that great conflict, the more it seems to be
clear that this was a war that none of the responsible
governments wanted; they just blundered into the car-
nage. It was set in motion by relatively trivial circumstances arising out of the assassination on a Sarajevo street
of Archduke Franz Ferdinand and his wife Sophie by the
terrorist Gavrilo Princip.

David Lloyd George wrote, "The more one reads of the memoirs and books written in the various countries of what happened before August 1, 1914, the more one realizes that no one at the head of affairs quite meant war. It was something into which they glided, or rather staggered and stumbled."

Once the automatic machinery of mobilization was set in motion, there was no way to reverse it and events had to grind on to their inevitable conclusion—10 million dead on the battlefield and twice that number wounded. The story is told that, after the war began, Prince Bülow, the former German Chancellor, asked the then Chancellor Bethmann-Hollweg, "How did it all happen?" The reply was, "Ah, if only one knew."

6

The Greatest Menace

World War II also has a very important lesson for our times, because the peculiar horror of our age is that the new atomic weapons can, for the first time in history, arm madmen so that they can act out their savage dreams in real life. This holds true for the madmen of small countries as well as those of large ones. Imagine if either Hitler or Stalin or Mussolini had atomic bombs at his disposal. Imagine all the other madmen of history, such as Julius Caesar or Genghis Khan or Napoleon, whose fame rests not so much on their victories or defeats as in the frightful number of their victims. For that matter, why should it be assumed that the men who create and control the monstrous modern-day nuclear devices are in their right minds?

Yet, President Johnson has truly said, "It used to be said that the hand that rocks the cradle is the hand that rules the world. Today, the hand that pushes the button is the hand that could destroy the world." In the last analysis, therefore, the greatest menace of accidental war arises from the quirks of personalities in high places. For example, Milovan Djilas in *Conversations with Stalin* asks "how such a dark, cunning and cruel individual could ever have led one of the greatest and most powerful states, not for just a day or a year, but for thirty years."

Today is not a time for greatness in our leadership, for men who seek to actively make a name for themselves in history. What we need now is not statesmanship, but lifemanship. Today is not a time for adventurers, brigands, pygmies, stiff-backed politicians, or bantam roosters strutting in our corridors of power. In a nuclear world the cost of bold leadership comes too high. The blood of the peoples of the world runs cold when our leaders call for action—any kind of action; any move to get the motors going. A chillness descends upon us when we hear our officials orate about defending national grandeur, national glory, national dignity, sacred honor—"To quit groveling and start acting like a world power." It doesn't seem to matter that all this is in violation of the United Nations Charter, under which terms no country is permitted to use force to protect its national honor.

True, things will be dull without the men of destiny who dreamed of power and glory and who added a sense of flair and drama to our otherwise drab lives. But such drama enacted in the grand manner on the world stage may be too great a luxury in this atomic age and the price of admission for the citizen may be much too high. The damage that Hitler and Stalin and Napoleon had wrought could, in time, be undone; and Lincoln, at worst, could lose only the Union. Today, the activist, triggered by emotion, could be absolutely disastrous for mankind. Today is rather a time for reflection, compassion and understanding.

Now, we have the word of no less an authority than Dr. Leo Szilard that chairman Khrushchev clearly grasped the essential nature of nuclear weapons. He was not officially characterized as "paranoic, capricious, irresponsible, harebrained, immature and hasty" until some time later. What of his successors, Brezhnev and Kosygin? We won't know until they, in turn, are displaced. The very anarchic, apparatchik nature of power transfer in the Soviet Union adds an ominous note of instability and danger to the world.

Dr. Ralph E. Lapp believes that "China can, in a very few years, become the most dangerous nuclear power of all—not because the Chinese leaders can match the United States might, but because they do not seem to understand nuclear war and, therefore, may not be rationally deterred from starting one." Chairman Mao told a visiting Yugoslav in 1957, "We aren't afraid of atomic bombs. What if they killed even 300 million? We would still have plenty more—China would be the last country to die." He told Khrushchev in 1963, "Can one guess how great will be the toll of human casualties in a future war? Possibly it would be a third of the 2.7 billion inhabitants of the entire world. . . . Personally, I think that, in the entire world, half of humanity, and perhaps even more than half, will perish. If half of humanity were destroyed, the other half would still remain, but imperialism would be destroyed entirely and there would be only socialism in all the world, and within half a century or a whole century the population would again increase by more than half."

There have been disturbing reports that Mao is obsessed

with the fear that the younger generation is too soft, never having fought a war, and thus might betray his revolution. He still holds to his famous thesis, "Political power grows out of the barrel of a gun." An often quoted passage from Mao's book *Problems of War and Strategy* states, "The seizure of power by armed forces, the settlement of an issue by war, is the central task and the highest form of Revolution."

An official statement of the Chinese Communist party on September 6, 1963 declared, "We say that if imperialism should unleash a nuclear war and the worst came to worst, half of the world's population would be killed. We are optimistic about the future of mankind." In 1965 Jenmin Jih Pao covered two pages with a statement by Marshal Lo Jui-ching, the former chief of the Chinese general staff. Writing of war in the nuclear age, he said that while such a conflict will "cause sacrifices and destruction, it will also educate the people" and will, in the end, be "turned from a bad thing to a good thing, accelerating the historical progress." He added that psychological preparation of the Chinese masses for nuclear war "must be given first priority."

In a major doctrinal article published September 3, 1965, Marshal Lin Piao, Chinese Defense Minister and heir apparent, wrote, "War can temper the people and push history forward. In this sense, war is a great school." He goes on to declare, "The spiritual atom bomb that the revolutionary people possess is a far more powerful and useful weapon than the physical atom bomb."

Chou En-lai was once asked if he did not think everything must be done to avoid the suffering caused by war. He replied that, on the contrary, it was by war that big things were achieved, that China had become what it is today as a result of invasion, destruction, famine, flood, pestilence and suffering.

Since nuclear deterrence ultimately depends upon a state of mind, the unbelievably dangerous delusion harbored by Mao Tse-tung and his men, that China might survive a nuclear war, poses a real threat to the security of the world. A nation that can seriously publish a dissertation entitled, "Defeat Atomic Bombs with Bayonets" as an important interpretation of "Chairman Mao's military thinking" is a menace to the peace of the world. Listen to Mao: "I personally like international tension. . . . There is a Chinese saying, 'People dare to touch the tiger's whiskers' and that is why one should not be afraid of international tension."

This writer has been plagued with a recurrent nightmare ever since Communist China detonated its first atomic bomb. In this dream, the Chinese, seeking revenge against both the United States and the Soviet Union, dispatch two nuclear-armed submarines into the Atlantic Ocean. One submarine lofts its missiles in the direction of America, the other eastward toward Russia.

There were times when one felt that President Kennedy understood the character of nuclear weapons. What about President Johnson? Can a man, who has been described as "vain, stubborn and parochially minded"; as "the greatest pragmatist of all time"; as "earthy, changeable and fiercely human"; as subject to "the most extreme swings between tenderness and cruelty, between dedication and cynicism, between comedy and high purpose"; as "obsessed with self"; as "insensitive to others, mean and irascible" be trusted with the thunderbolt of nuclear power?

The quixotic figure of le grand Charles, General de

Gaulle, is a throwback to the age of the national swash-buckler. Responsible military authorities are of the pre-vailing opinion that the force de frappé is most inefficient, useless in defense, both in retaliation and as deterrent. Then why has a thrifty France committed billions of francs of its hard-earned horde to the meaningless sym-bol. General Paul Gérardot offered the answer in *Le Monde* of February 2, 1955: "Do we want France to possess, as is possible, the modern and effective atomic arm which can guarantee the defense of its independence and sovereignty? . . . If we do not want to produce the indispensable nuclear arms, it is a waste of time to speak about French independence, for economic and political independence do not exist without a minimum of military independence." President de Gaulle sent the following cablegram of congratulations upon the explosion of France's first atomic bomb in 1960: "Hurrah for France! Since this morning she is stronger and prouder."

Can it be that our leaders have learned nothing from this bloodstained century? Can it be that international relations are still only an expression of rivalry between peacocks where bombs are to the protagonists what feath-ers are to the peacock, and where atomic bomb rattling is just feather preening? Then why do our heads of state continue to hold international intercourse largely in the language of genocide, with incessant talk of building more destructive weapons, extending their potential use, manip-ulating them in a game of threat and counter-threat? Could it be that our leaders have adopted the dictum of the poet Rilke that "danger has become safer than secu-rity"—or if not danger, its aura?

Lord Boyd Orr posed the all-important question of the

day: "The all-important question is whether the relatively few men who control the destiny of the present changing civilization have the political maturity, the wisdom and the goodwill to initiate the great international creative effort needed to bring the new epoch into being, or whether in their short-sighted pride of power, they will attempt to apply obsolete means, which will destroy the present civilization."

Based upon all experience and every evidence of history, we must reply, in all candor, that the answer will undoubtedly be destruction of the present civilization. Oxenstierna, who was Chancellor to King Gustav Adolphus of Sweden some 300 years ago, reflected in his old age on the Thirty Years' War that had ravaged Europe and said: "My son, my son, if you knew with what little wisdom the world is ruled." Indeed, a study of the history of statesmanship must conclude that governments, in the main, are deeply criminal.

It would be most difficult to convince our leaders that the happy days of successful slaughter have been brought to an end. Although we feel that an immense military establishment is a threat to the fabric of our civilization, we make extraordinary demands upon our leaders when we call for disarmament. As Thomas Paine remarked almost 200 years ago: "To establish any mode to abolish war, however advantageous it might be to nations, would be to take from such governments the most lucrative of its branches."

Perhaps Bertrand Russell's dire evaluation of the leadership of the atomic era is more on target than we dare to admit: "The leaders of the modern world are drunk with power. The fact that they can do something no one else thought it possible to do is to them a sufficient reason for doing it." The epitaph to our age may well be the same as that of the age of the dinosaurs: too much armor, too little brain.

What makes the conduct of international affairs by our leaders so ominous is the almost complete abdication by the people of their responsibilities. They don't ask any more; they don't criticize. They accept. The principle that the people have the right to know—the right to be informed—has been abrogated. Our leaders express poorly concealed contempt for those who dare to question our all-powerful government. Governments have no opponents—only enemies. Reason becomes treason.

Information is blatantly manipulated as just another weapon in a nation's military arsenal. The government defends its inherent right "to lie" to save "itself when it's going up into a nuclear war." The possibility that the people might have to die by the millions does not appear important enough to warrant piercing the veil of government by secrecy. By a bizarre twist of logic, vital information is withheld from the public in the public interest.

For example, a film entitled *The War Game* which portrayed in documentary style what might happen to the County of Kent if it was devastated by Soviet bombs, was banned from television by the British Broadcasting Corporation as "too horrifying." Or was the real reason the one stated by the writer-director, Peter Watkins, that it was an attempt to suppress the film which sought to expose the "silence on why we possess nuclear weapons" and "to make men in the street stop and think about himself and his future."

Chief executives (including President Kennedy) do not hesitate to exert pressure to secure the reassignment of reporters who write uncomfortable stories. They agree with Napoleon who complained that "Three hostile newspapers are more to be feared than a thousand bayonets." Professor H. Stuart Hughes concludes, "I doubt whether in the history of modern democracy there has ever been so yawning a gap between the official story and the reality, between public rhetoric and private knowledge."

Good examples of this public rhetoric are the so-called "missile gap" of the 1960's and the so-called "bomber gap" of the 1950's which never were. Another is the "manpower gap" between the NATO forces and the Russian hordes. First, it was claimed that the Red Army comprised 150 divisions. Only after it was demonstrated that such strength was mathematically impossible, given the population statistics, was it conceded that perhaps Western manpower did actually exceed the Soviet numbers. Paul H. Nitze, the Assistant Secretary of Defense, disclosed to the Cleveland Council on World Affairs, on March 2, 1963, that the NATO powers had 5.8 million men under arms compared to the 4.3 million for the Warsaw pact countries. C. L. Sulzberger commented in the *New York Times* of December 2, 1963: "Somewhere, Khrushchev seems to have lost 100 divisions."

An incident of the Vietnam war offers a prime instance of official deception. In August 1964, U Thant, the Secretary General of the United Nations, had formally conveyed to the United States government an offer by North Vietnam to meet in Rangoon, Burma, to discuss terms for ending hostilities. This offer was rejected by the United States government.

Perhaps because of the election campaign and the Administration's pose as the peace party, perhaps for other reasons, the United States government went to great lengths to conceal the offer and its rejection from the American people. The President's press secretary, George Reedy, denied that any proposal had been received from U. Thant. President Johnson himself, as late as a press conference, on July 13, 1965, insisted, "I must say that candor compels me to tell you that there has not been the slightest indication that the other side is interested in negotiation or in unconditional discussions, although the United States has made some dozen separate attempts to bring that about." Candor, indeed!

Or, consider the half-truths divulged to secure passage of the Tonkin Gulf Resolution which became "the functional equivalent" of a declaration of war against North Vietnam and justification for the bombing of that nation. A post-mortem held by the Senate Foreign Relations Committee, more than three years after the fact, disclosed that the North Vietnamese gunboat forays against the *Maddox* and the *Turner Joy* on August 2 and 4, 1964 were not completely "unprovoked" and that these destroyers were not "carrying out a routine patrol of the type we carry out all over the world at all times."

As a matter of fact, the two vessels were spy ships and they had been involved in the South Vietnamese actions against the islands of Hon Me and Hon Nieu. Further, the commander of the *Maddox*, Captain John J. Herrick, sent the following cable to Washington on August 4, the day of the second alleged incident: "A review of action makes many reported contacts and torpedoes fired appear doubtful. Freak weather effects and over-eager sonarmen may have accounted for reports. No visual sightings by *Maddox*. Suggest further evaluation before any further action."

But without waiting for such an evaluation, President

Johnson, on the next day, August 5, ordered the first air strikes against North Vietnam and, at the same time, asked the Senate to pass the resolution which adviser McGeorge Bundy had drafted far in advance and had even cleared with the South Vietnamese government.

Was the late Admiral Kimmel really insane when he suggested that President Franklin D. Roosevelt, having broken the Japanese code, was aware of the impending attack on Pearl Harbor but said nothing because he wanted the United States in the war?

The result is, on the one hand, a crisis of credibility in spoon-fed information and, on the other hand, a default of the decision-making power in international affairs to the leaders who supposedly have the facts. The masses are shunted towards the Scharnhorst ideal of implicit, mindless obedience—a sort of panicky, degrading leader-worship of the self-assured captains of the hour who strut about among us in the jingling harnesses of their success and importance. Representative government by the consent of the governed becomes meaningless when those who are governed do not even know to what they are consenting.

The potential for the disastrous use of power is serious enough when this power is exercised by a small legally constituted group at the center. The danger becomes intolerable when misplaced power in the formulation and in the execution of foreign policy is assumed by the invisible government, comprised of the various secret intelligence agencies of the different nations. These agencies, answerable to no one, engage in their back-alley struggle in the utmost secrecy, without the knowledge of other government departments, and often without adequate reporting to the chief executive or legislative authorities.

The United States Central Intelligence Agency, for example, has acted on its own, as a superstate, in Cuba, Iran, the Congo, Indonesia, Guatemala, Greece, the Dominican Republic, Singapore, Burma, Cambodia, Vietnam, and elsewhere. At home, the C.I.A. has subsidized in secret and subverted any number of voluntary student, labor, research, study, and civic organizations. In the words of Congressman Benjamin S. Rosenthal, "It is intolerable that intelligence activities of the Central Intelligence Agency and other organizations are free from democratic review." It is reliably reported that President Kennedy was not informed in advance of the planned *coup d'état* of November 1-2, 1963 to overthrow South Vietnam's President Ngo Dinh Diem. Even a President, being human, can spread his attention span over only a limited number of problems. Admittedly, President Kennedy had never given "his full attention" to the problem of Vietnam. The invisible government stepped into the power vacuum left by official government.

The Bible tells the stories of the stopping of the sun in the heavens, of the parting of the waters, and of all the other great miracles wrought by God. By now, the citizen must have realized that no miracle can possibly compare with the fact that an atomic bomb has not slipped since 1945 and blown the earth to bits. For this wonder, that we are still here, each of us should give prayerful thanks every day. But the Good Lord must be growing increasingly impatient with the squabbling little people who are squandering their allotted time. There is no guarantee that the miracle will carry over into tomorrow or the day after.

7

The Story of Disarmament—
Pre-Atomic Era

Here is another puzzlement for the citizen. Today, as was the case prior to 1914 and 1939, we are assured by our leaders that the application of the para bellum doctrine (called deterrence today and by other names in earlier periods) is guaranteed to maintain the peace. We are also assured that an elaborate and foolproof command and control system makes accidental war impossible. If this is the case, then how do we explain the frantic around-the-calendar disarmament conferences which are in session today and have been in session almost continuously since the beginning of the century? Aren't these disarmament conferences in themselves an admission that the hatches against war have not been battened down so snugly as we have been led to believe? Or are the disarmament sessions simply a sop to quiet the woolly-headed peace agitators in our midst?

This chapter and the next will seek to formulate an answer to these questions.

Now what is a disarmament conference and how does it come into being and how does it go about its business? In essence, it is an exercise in diplomacy—the traditional, time-honored way of conducting relations between nations. Upon the initiative of one or more heads of government, it is agreed that designated plenipotentiaries of these heads will convene together at a certain time, at a certain place. Once assembled, they sit down around the traditional green felt table and they negotiate about the levels of armaments permitted to each participating nation.

There have been other, far more caustic, characterizations of the processes of diplomacy. The important factor to remember is that the diplomats are not free agents, but representatives of their kings or their governments. Chairman Khrushchev once said of Soviet Foreign Minister Andrei Gromyko, "He would sit on a cake of ice with his pants down until I tell him to get up." The diplomats must always be careful, therefore, to defend jealously the majesty of their sovereigns and to hew closely to their instructions. We can now begin to understand Rousseau's description of an international conference "where we deliberate in common council whether the table will be round or square, whether the hall will have more doors or less, whether such and such a plenipotentiary will have his face or back turned toward the window." As a matter of fact, at the Congress of Vienna, which followed the Napoleonic wars, Count Metternich cut three additional doors in the conference room at Belvedere Palace so that each of the plenipotentiaries could make a simultaneous entrance.

The diplomats resemble most the troubadours of old who wandered from court to court extolling the praises and the might of their feudal lords. Their concern is not so much to further the business of the convocation as it is to gratify the emotions back home. They come together not so much for the purpose of settling their differences by negotiation as to tell each other how powerful they are.

They do so because they know their job well. In the same way that God marches on the side of the strongest battalions, the merits of international negotiations rest with the most powerful nations. It was Frederick the Great who said that diplomacy without armaments was like music without instruments. Thus inferior armed strength is reflected not only in defeats on the battlefield but also in concessions at the council table. This truism is particularly relevant in the nuclear age. Never before have unused weapons weighed so heavily in the discussions among nations.

In discussing the diplomacy of violence, it is interesting to note that Urs Schwartz, of the *Neue Zürcher Zeitung,* believes that political-military thinking in the United States has achieved a Clausewitzian breakthrough. He argues that "American strategic thought has by now overcome the reluctance to admit power (including nuclear power) as an element of national policy" to accomplish the objectives defined by that policy.

The outcome of international conferences is determined more by the respective size of the military establishment than by the eloquence or logic of the diplomats. All the grand talk about justice and peace is simply the sentimental balderdash with which the strong seek to palliate their aggression and the weak to camouflage their inferiority. The French Foreign Minister Waleski remarked

to Bismarck that the task of the diplomat was to cloak
the selfish interests of his country in the language of universal justice. The only legitimate test as to which of two
sides of an international quarrel is right is to ask which
is the stronger.

Thus, the purpose of international diplomacy is to cod-
ify the relative strength of the powers at any given
moment. Since the status is always shifting, no international treaty can hope to continue in force for too long
a time. When an imbalance of force exists between the
negotiators, or where there is a difference of judgment
as to what the true distribution of power really is, the
situation is not objectively negotiable. It can only be
submitted to the ultimate arbitrament of war.

The age old tradition of diplomacy formally ratifies the
age old law of the jungle that the strong shall take what
they can and the weak shall grant what they must. Wise
Winston Churchill knew of what he spoke when he wrote,
"We arm to parley." Thus, it was in perfect accordance
with protocol for the United States to call for an all-out
effort to win the war in three months at the same time
that it was beginning the Paris talks with North Vietnam.
If all this sounds unspeakably amoral and cynical, this
writer need only refer the reader to the history of diplomacy. He must come away with Stalin's conclusion that
"a sincere diplomat is no more possible than iron wood."

These are the ground rules. Now for the history of disarmament negotiations. The first real full dress disarmament conference was the Hague Conference of 1899. Prior
to that time, there had been some feeble groping towards
disarmament. In 1766, Chancellor Kaunitz of Austria had
suggested a proportionate reduction of forces to Frederick

the Great of Prussia. A 1787 naval agreement between England and France provided for proportionate reduction of existing vessels of the line and limited the naval building program of both nations, but the rise of Napoleon prevented this treaty from becoming operative.

The only disarmament treaty that has remained in effect for any length of time was negotiated in 1817 between England and the United States. This was the Rush-Bagot Agreement which restricted the naval forces of each side on the Great Lakes and Lake Champlain to one armed vessel on Lake Champlain, one on Lake Ontario, and two on the upper lakes, with one eighteen-pound gun allowed to each vessel. The 1871 Anglo-American Treaty of Washington extended the defortification to the Canadian land frontier.

In March 1816, Alexander I of Russia wrote to His Holy Alliance partner Lord Castlereagh proposing a general reduction of armed forces. Castlereagh communicated this proposal to the third ally, Count Metternich. The latter's reply sounds strangely familiar: he rejected the idea saying that because of the "difficulty always of obtaining any true data from Russia . . . to take the initiative here, uncertain of a reciprocity of confidence, would be impossible."

Napoleon III, in his speech from the throne on November 5, 1863, bewailed, "Are we, with our excessive armaments, to maintain an attitude of mutual defiance indefinitely? Must our most precious resources be forever wasted in a vain ostentation of force? Shall we forever maintain a state of affairs which is neither peace with security nor war." There is no record of anyone having paid any attention to this wail. Indeed, Napoleon III himself soon forgot about it when he launched upon his adventures in Mexico.

The St. Petersburg declaration of 1868 which followed the Austro-Hungarian-Prussian War of 1866 prohibited "the use of weapons of mass destruction causing unnecessary human suffering."

August 24, 1898, was the occasion for a truly magnificent and eloquent appeal addressed to the nations of the world on behalf of reason, law, disarmament and peace in international relations. This appeal took the form of an Imperial Rescript issued in the name of Nicholas II, the Czar of all the Russians. The rescript read as follows: "In the course of the last twenty years the longings for a general appeasement have been especially pronounced in the consciousness of civilized nations. The preservation of peace has been put forward as the object of international policy; in its name, great States have concluded between themselves powerful alliances; it is the better to guarantee peace that they have developed, in proportion hitherto unprecedented, their military forces and still continue to increase them without shrinking from any sacrifice.

"All these efforts, nevertheless, have not been able to bring about the beneficent results of the desired pacification. . . . The intellectual and physical strength of the nations are for the major part diverted from their natural application and unproductively consumed. Hundreds of millions are devoted to acquiring terrible engines of destruction which, though today regarded as the last word of science, are destined tomorrow to lose all value in consequence of some fresh discovery in the same field. Moreover, the armaments less and less fulfill the objects which the governments have set themselves. The economic crises, due in great part to the system of armaments à l'outrance, and the continued danger which lies in this massing of war material, are transforming the armed peace of our days into a crushing burden, which the peoples have more and more difficulty in bearing.

"It appears evident that if this state of things were prolonged, it would inevitably lead to the very cataclysm which it is desired to avert, and the horrors of which make every thinking man shudder in advance. . . . To put an end to these incessant armaments is the supreme duty which is today imposed on all states."

The Czar went on to propose a conference of those states which "sincerely seek the triumph of the great concept of universal peace over the elements of trouble and disorder."

The proposed agenda included acceptance of the principle of arbitration in appropriate cases, the establishment of a tribunal for the mediation of disputes between nations, a two-year freeze of existing force levels and war budgets, and a prohibition on the use of new destabilizing terror weapons.

Some cynics say that Nicholas II had convoked the Hague Conference because his treasury was bankrupt and he realized that he was being left behind in the arms race by Austria-Hungary, Germany and Japan. But the fact is that, for the first time in centuries, the door was opened to the building of a new federation of nations which could make peace possible for humanity.

Some very worthwhile accomplishments emerged from the first Hague conference. The greatest accomplishment, of course, was the establishment of the Permanent Court of Arbitration at the Hague, which began to function in 1901. Conventions were adopted codifying international law, defining the customs of war to make the slaughter more polite, providing for discretionary arbitration of international disputes, and prohibiting the use of inhuman weapons. The latter included, among others, dum-dum bullets, bombs dropped from balloons, and shells containing gas.

It is interesting to note that the United States refused to ratify the Hague Convention "to abstain from the use of projectiles the sole object of which is the diffusion of asphyxiating or deleterious gases." This negative action was taken on the advice of the American delegate to the conference Captain (later Admiral) Alfred Thayer Mahan who explained that such weapons could "produce decisive results." In the light of this stand, it is a little difficult to understand the American outcry over the first use of poison gas at Ypres on April 22, 1915.

The United States representation at this first of the great international disarmament conferences illustrates another fact of life of these meetings. Anthony Nutting, who has had wide experience in this area, explains it: "The student of this melancholy piece of history [disarmament negotiation] must always bear in mind—as the negotiators for their part were never allowed to forget—that behind each disarmament delegation there hovers that gaunt grey giant in the counsels of men and nations—the Ministry of Defence." Thus, in order for the citizen to understand the disarmament negotiations which we will be discussing, it would be well for him to occasionally lift his eyes from the green felt tables, around which the soft, quiet, courteous voices are purring in correct, exactly measured phrases. He might then discern the delicate wires which lead from the puppets sitting at the table to the military brass hovering protectively overhead.

A second Hague conference, at which forty-four nations were represented, convened in 1907 to further extend and strengthen the conventions adopted at the first meeting.

The fatal flaw of the Hague conferences was that the nations had been able to accomplish nothing with regard to the greatest challenge facing the gatherings—disarmament. It was this failure which was to cause the lights of Europe to go out one by one, not to be kindled again for four long years.

Viscount Grey of Fallodon, the foreign secretary of Great Britain, was to write in his memoirs: "The enormous growth of armaments in Europe, the sense of insecurity and fear caused by them—it was these that made war inevitable. This, it seems to me, is the truest reading of history and the lesson that the present should be learning from the past in the interests of future peace, the warning to be handed on to those who come after us.

"The increase of armaments, that is intended in each nation to produce consciousness of strength and a sense of security, does not produce these effects. On the contrary, it produces a consciousness of the strength of other nations and a sense of fear. Fear begets suspicion and distrust and evil imaginings of all sort, till each government feels it would be criminal not to take every precaution, while every government regards every precaution of every other government as evidence of hostile intent. . . .

"More than one true thing may be said about the causes of the war, but the statement that comprises most truth is that the military, and the armaments inseparable from it, made war inevitable. Armaments were intended to produce a sense of security in each nation. What they really did was to produce fear in everybody. Fear causes suspicion and hatred."

Point Four of Woodrow Wilson's Fourteen Points had called for "adequate guarantees given and taken that national armaments will be reduced to the lowest point consistent with domestic safety." The Treaty of Versailles, of course, provided for the disarmament of Germany. Before affixing their signatures to the treaty, the German delegation had written to the Big Three: "Germany is prepared to agree to her proposed disarmament provided this is a beginning of a general reduction of armaments." Premier Clemenceau replied, "The Allied and Associated Powers wish to make it clear that their requirements in regard to German armaments were not made solely with the object of rendering it impossible for her to resume her policy of military aggression. They are also the first step toward that general reduction and limitation of armaments which they seek to bring about as one of the most fruitful preventatives of war and which it will be one of the first duties of the League of Nations to promote."

The war to end war had ended. The guardianship over the affairs of men had passed into the hands of the League of Nations—albeit a League without the United States. Prime Minister Lloyd George prophesied, "Disarmament would be regarded as the real test of whether the League of Nations was a farce or whether business was meant."

Article 8 of the Charter required the League of Nations Council to formulate plans for arms reduction, and indeed one of the first actions of the League, in 1920, established the Temporary Mixed Commission for the Reduction of Armaments (TMC). The 1921 session of the League of Nations Assembly delineated the functions of this commission as recommended by the disarmament committee of the Assembly (of which Lord Robert Cecil was the *rapporteur*). The mandate covered formulation by the TMC of a definite scheme for disarmament, institution of steps dealing with the traffic in arms, and preparation of regulations concerning the private manufacture of munitions. A permanent section of the Secretariat was also created to deal with the question of disarmament.

But the TMC ran into trouble from its very beginning, because its members were appointed at large and were not representatives of the governments. This arrangement the various bureaucracies could not condone and finally, in 1925, the conservative British government refused to have anything further to do with the TMC.

The League had no alternative but to constitute another body, which was done at the Sixth Assembly in 1925. A resolution invited the Council to "proceed to preparatory studies for the organization of a conference with a view to the reduction and limitation of armaments, so that, once conditions satisfactory from the point of view of the General Secretariat are assured—the said conference be convoked and a general reduction and limitation of armaments carried out."

The Council set up a Committee of Studies under the presidency of J. Paul-Boncour. The report of this committee resulted in the appointment, in December, 1925, of a new group, which was called the Preparatory Commission for the Disarmament Conference, under the presidency of M. Loudon. It was charged with the responsibility of preparing an agenda and of issuing a call for a full-dress international disarmament conference.

The commission plodded along in the usual desultory fashion from May 1926 to December 1930, regurgitating ad nauseam the usual shopworn discussions about ratios, standing armies, reserves, offensive weapons, defensive weapons, inspection. The United States participated in the work of the commission from its inception and the Soviet Union joined the deliberations in 1927.

The only real stir in the humdrum sessions came on November 30, 1927, when the Soviet delegate, Maxim Litvinov, delivered his initial speech and called for complete and universal disarmament, with inspection, in the space of one year. One can imagine the resultant wave of shock and dismay that swept through the civilized world. It is interesting to note that the United States had already rejected the notion of inspection. Secretary of State Frank B. Kellogg had stated, on August 19, 1926, that his country "should not be subject to inspection or control by foreign agencies. Limitation must depend on good faith."

At long last, the call was sent out by the 1930 League of Nations Assembly for the convening of the Conference for the Reduction and Limitation of Armaments. The date was set for February 2, 1932. The World Disarmament Conference opened—with representatives of fifty-nine nations, including the United States, in attendance—in an atmosphere of crisis: Japan had invaded Manchuria on September 18, 1931. The Women's International League for Peace and Freedom—the theme of whose seventh congress at Grenoble had been "world disarmament or world disaster"—presented a petition containing eight million

signatures to the president of the disarmament conference, Arthur Henderson.

In opening the conference, the former British foreign
secretary declared, "I refuse to contemplate even the possibility of failure; but if we fail, no one can foretell the
evil consequences that might ensue." Among the proposals
forwarded to the conference, President Herbert Hoover
first suggested the outlawry of all armaments capable of
being used for offensive purposes. He later was willing to
settle for a 30 per cent across the board cut in forces above
a fixed police level and abolition of horror weapons, such
as tanks, large mobile guns, bombing planes, and instruments of chemical warfare. But there were still no takers.

Litvinov again attacked the hypocrisy of the capitalist
powers and exposed the dilatoriness and humbug of the
disarmament proceedings. He renewed his plea for universal disarmament subject to "very rigorous supervision."
That stuff was old hat by then and no one paid too much
attention. France insisted that security must precede disarmament and wanted an international police force first.

So the great world disarmament conference dragged
along, holding meetings until June 16, 1934, although the
Conference Bureau continued in existence until May 31,
1937. Germany had withdrawn from the conference in
1934. The sound of the proceedings was being drowned
out by the thud of the hob-nailed boots of the Japanese,
the Nazis and the Fascists, in China, in Ethiopia, in Albania, in the Rhineland, in the Sudetenland and elsewhere. Sir Winston Churchill summed up the work of the
conference—"a solemn and prolonged farce."

The many treatises by the scholars and authorities on
the great 1932 world disarmament conference serve as an

object lesson for the reader. The experts painstakingly pore over each incident of the conference, lamenting upon how things would have been different of only this or that had occurred.

For instance, Philip Noel-Baker, Nobel Peace Prize laureate and an outstanding authority in the field of disarmament, writes in his book *The Arms Race*, "The League Disarmament Conference was not doomed to futility from the start. It failed, indeed; but if Sir John Simon had succeeded in persuading the British cabinet to accept President Hoover's proposals of June, 1932; if Mr. Stanley Baldwin had beaten Lord Londonderry more swiftly and decisively in the long drawn cabinet struggle about the abolition of the bomber; if Sir Anthony Eden's belated Draft Convention of March 1933 had been put forward a year earlier; it might have had a rapid and notable success."

If . . . if . . . if. One loses the forest for the trees. By now, the reader of this book will know that this great conference—like all other conferences—was doomed to futility from the start—because it lacked, from the start, the will to succeed.

In the meantime, other disarmament meetings were going on elsewhere—both outside and under the auspices of the League of Nations. In the long history of disarmament, outside of the Rush-Bagot agreement, only two very partial successes can be recorded. One of these is the 1922 Washington Naval Treaty on naval limitations. This treaty limited total tonnage in capital ships and aircraft carriers for Great Britain, the United States, Japan, France, and Italy to ratios of 5:5:3:1.75 respectively. In addition, there was to be a ten-year naval holiday on capital ships and aircraft carriers, and the size of the armaments on warships was to be limited. Perhaps the naval treaties were possible because the great battleships were already obsolete.

President Calvin Coolidge issued a call for a second naval conference, which convened in Geneva in 1927. Unfortunately, this conference proved abortive because the British conservative government repudiated the agreement which had been negotiated by its delegation headed by Lord Robert Cecil. As a result, Lord Cecil resigned from the government because he thought the United States had been treated as a rival and a potential enemy. He wrote in his memoirs, "It was quite wrong to treat the question as if we and the Americans were enemies, if not actual, at least possible."

The third naval conference, held in London in 1930, was more successful. The London Naval Treaty also limited the total tonnage of British, American and Japanese cruisers, destroyers and submarines. Also, the naval holiday was extended until 1936. By that time, it was all wholly academic.

Another important treaty of this period was the Protocol for the Prohibition of the Use in War of Asphyxiating, Poisonous or Other Gases and of Bacteriological Methods of Warfare concluded at Geneva on June 17, 1925. Forty-two nations adhered to this treaty banning the use of gas in warfare as "condemned by a consensus of the civilized world." The United States again refused to ratify.

We must not forget the Kellogg-Briand Pact of 1928 under the terms of which sixty-two countries solemnly outlawed war forever as an instrument of international policy.

The pre-1939 world, given the choice between world disarmament and world disaster, chose world disaster. The price for mistakes in international affairs runs inordinately high. This time it cost 33 million dead. Next time?

8

The Story of Disarmament— Atomic Era

World Was II ended with those awesome blasts at Hiroshima and Nagasaki, with "the light of many suns in one"—"a light not of this world." A new world had dawned, one so completely different from the old, with such an overwhelming and shattering import, that the future would be tolled as years of the atomic era instead of the Christian era.

In the glare of this terrible new light, did humanity disenthrall itself from the old ways of thinking and behavior? With armaments no longer conventional, what of the thinking? Albert Einstein offered the answer, "The splitting of the atom has changed everything save our modes of thinking and thus we drift toward unparalleled catastrophe."

And in the glare of this new light, did the diplomats return to the conference table with a new spirit of determination to save the world from another disaster? Did they return purged of the old cynical presumption that the adversary harbored only the worst possible motives? Did they disabuse themselves of the old notion that a willingness to negotiate was a sign of weakness?

The record will show that the diplomats returned only to resume business as usual. They unbuckled their old six-shooters, rested them on the table, and resumed the old-fashioned international poker game. They nestled comfortably back into the old pre-nuclear days when megaton bombs were unheard of, the cavalry still paraded, and national sovereignty was absolute. Ignoring the lateness of the hour and the rapid pace of the new era, the whole antiquated machinery of courtly diplomacy was reinstalled in the vaulted palaces. The plenipotentiaries in their cutaways resumed the old stately diplomatic minuet in the mode of nineteenth-century balance-of-power politics. The bowls of jelly, constantly smiling, unembarrassed by banalities, resumed their cloaks of imperturbable, unimaginative blandness. The talkathon continued from where it had been broken off as if nothing had changed.

The new era opened with the legacy of the promises which had been held out by the Four Freedoms and the Atlantic Charter. Franklin D. Roosevelt had explained: "The fourth is freedom from fear—which translated into world terms, means a world-wide reduction of armaments to such a point and in such a fashion that no nation will be in a position to commit an act of physical aggression against any neighbor—anywhere in the world."

The Atlantic Charter of August 14, 1941, had declared: "Eighth, they believe that all the nations of the world, for realistic as well as spiritual reasons, must come to the abandonment of the use of force. Since no future peace can be maintained if land, sea or air armaments continue to be employed by nations which threaten, or may threaten, aggression outside of their frontiers, they believe, pending the establishment of a wide and permanent system of general security, that the disarmament of such nations is essential. They will likewise aid and encourage all other practicable measures which will lighten for peace loving peoples the crushing burden of armaments."

The United Nations Charter—in one sense an obsolete document even before it came into force on June 25, 1945, because it was a pre-atomic age charter—refers to "disarmament" only three times: Article II states, "The General Assembly may consider the general principle of cooperation in the maintenance of international peace and security, including the principles governing disarmament and the regulation of armaments, and may make recommendations with regard to such principles to the Members or to the Security Council or to both."

Article 26 provides: "In order to promote the extension and maintenance of international peace and security with the least diversion for armaments of the world's human and economic resources, the Security Council shall be responsible for formulation, with the assistance of the Military Staff Committee referred to in Article 47, plans to be submitted to the Members of the United Nations for the establishment of a system for the regulation of armaments." Article 47 merely follows through and authorizes the Military Staff Committee to advise the Security Council on "regulation of armaments and possible disarmament."

Little time was lost before the United Nations Atomic Energy Commission was organized on January 24, 1946, through the very first resolution approved by the General Assembly. The stage was set for Bernard Baruch to make his "quick and the dead" speech and to present the Acheson-Baruch-Lilienthal plan to the Commission on June 14, 1946.

It must be remembered that the United States at this time had a monopoly of atomic weapons—a unique global advantage without parallel in recorded history. It thus was a most magnanimous gesture of unexampled generosity for this nation to offer to destroy its entire stockpile of atomic weapons. This was conditioned upon the prior establishment and functioning of a United Nations International Atomic Development Authority with an adequate veto-free system for control and "condign punishment" of violators.

After that date, all stores of Uranium and Thorium and all uses of these metals and their derivatives would pass under the control and ownership of the international agency. Representatives of this authority would have freedom of access to carry out inspections anywhere in the world and illegal possession, use or manufacture of atomic materials would be severely penalized. The veto power would not be effective in the application of sanctions for infringements of the control agreement. In the meantime, of course, all other nations would be barred from producing atomic weapons.

But was the United States really so magnanimous? Andrei Gromyko wanted to know why the stockpile of bombs could not be destroyed before controls were instituted. He asked why the Soviet Union should trust the

United States to disarm at the proper time when the American insistence on inspection showed that they didn't trust the Russians. He asked why it was necessary for the United States to wait until the last possible moment before divesting itself of bombs—especially when atomic power was being turned over to an agency which was controlled by the United States, and which it hoped to continue to control. He pointed out that the United States would retain a monopoly of the atomic knowhow and that this knowledge would be denied to everyone else. Mr. Baruch replied that the United States "must have a guarantee of safety."

In retrospect, the Acheson-Baruch-Lilienthal Plan, despite its seeming boldness and generosity, seems curiously naïve. What it amounted to was an attempt by the West to snatch a permanent political advantage through exploitation of a temporary atomic superiority. As a matter of fact, the United States, despite repeated urging, never did come forward with a time schedule for the institution of control and the surrender of its atomic arsenal. The United States tried to bluff the Soviet Union into accepting a state of permanent atomic inferiority and it failed.

Questions have even been raised by Gar Alperovitz as to whether the bombs were dropped on Japan in order to shorten that war or in order to serve as an object lesson to the Russians. How else can one explain the dropping of the bomb on Nagasaki, with a loss of 70,000 lives, only three days after the Hiroshima bomb? Suppose the shoe had been on the other foot and the Soviet Union had a monopoly of atomic power, would the United States have acceded to an Acheson-Baruch-Lilienthal plan?

The answer came at the sixth General Assembly session

in Paris in 1951. Bernard Baruch had resigned in late 1946 in protest over the State Department's insistence on suspension of the veto in atomic questions. The actual work of the United Nations Atomic Energy Commission had ended on May 17, 1948. The Soviet Union had exploded its atomic bomb in September 1949. The Vinson mission, which had been dispatched to Moscow by President Truman to break the conference deadlock, had failed. Under these circumstances, the United States formally abandoned the Acheson-Baruch-Lilienthal plan and moved that the General Assembly terminate the work of the Commission.

At this point, the Soviet delegation suddenly reversed its demand that American atomic bombs must be destroyed first. Mr. Vishinsky belatedly accepted the American single-package idea and suggested simultaneous conclusion of two conventions: one outlawing atomic weapons and one establishing control mechanisms. This reversal of position was, of course, denounced as an "Asiatic maneuver" and suspension of the Commission was finally voted by the General Assembly.

One has the feeling that President Truman was never too happy with the Acheson-Baruch-Lilienthal plan. Perhaps this explains the reluctance with which the plan was advanced and the take it or leave it attitude in which it was debated. President Truman probably favored the notion of American trusteeship over atomic power that he had expressed in his 1945 Navy Day speech.

The debate over the Acheson-Baruch-Lilienthal plan has been set forth in some detail because it presents in microcosm the story of disarmament negotiation in the atomic era. It illustrates an important principle that the reader should keep in mind. That principle is never to volunteer to give up what you have; always give up what the other fellow has. Or, if the other side doesn't have it yet, then try to fix it so that he can never acquire it. Only offer to give up what has outlived its usefulness for you or what you have so much of that the glut is coming out of your ears.

Sir Winston Churchill relates a fable of disarmament in the zoo. The rhinoceros wants to outlaw the use of teeth, which he claims is barbarous, while he holds that horns are defensive weapons. The leopard maintains that teeth are merely utensils for mastication while the hug is the really horrible weapon. The bear then rises to his full height on his hind legs and says, "How ridiculous can you be. Everyone knows that the hug is a fraternal gesture. The claw is the real . . ."

In more civilized societies, the nations that have atomic weapons see the real threat in proliferation of these devices, while at the same time they make no offer to reduce their own stockpiles. Countries with smaller populations point to the danger of great land armies. States without foreign bases belive that the great peril lies there. Open societies call for inspection; closed societies call inspection espionage.

Once the citizen has grasped the principles of disarmament negotiations, it would seem almost superfluous to recite here the futile and melancholy gestures toward negotiation dating from the Baruch Plan to the present. But, after all, this is supposed to be a book about disarmament and it is only proper that a brief review of this dreary history be recorded here.

We have already mentioned the United Nations Atomic

Energy Commission which was composed of the members of the Security Council and Canada. This agency, as we have seen, made no progress whatever because the Soviet Union would not agree to the Acheson-Baruch-Lilienthal Plan and the United States would not agree to the Soviet demand that the atomic stockpile be destroyed first. To parallel the work of this group, a Commission for Conventional Armaments had been constituted on February 13, 1947, comprised of the members of the Security Council.

To this latter Commission the West proposed that a ceiling be put on armed forces so that the United States, China and the Soviet Union would be limited to one million men each, with a smaller amount for Britain and France. It should be remembered here that the United States had disbanded its armies in great haste after World War II and had brought its men home. The Soviets countered with the statement that the same diet should be good for the fat man as the thin man and suggested instead a one-third across the board reduction in both manpower and armaments. This Commission, too, reached a stalemate because to discuss conventional forces, without regard to atomic power, was like playing cards with a deck stripped of aces.

To resolve the stalemate, the 1951 General Assembly appointed a committee of four representing the Soviet Union, the United States, France, and Great Britain. This committee proposed that the Atomic Energy Commission and the Conventional Armaments Commission be merged into a Disarmament Committee of the eleven members of the Security Council and Canada. This committee became operative on January 11, 1952. The Western powers had proposed to the third General Assembly a census of armed forces and armaments—*excluding* atomic weapons —and this plan had been voted in November 1948. The Western powers now renewed this proposal to the new committee.

The Western program was (a) divulgence by a census and verification of conventional armed forces and armaments, (b) a balanced reduction of these conventional armed forces and armaments and (c) a prohibition of weapons of mass destruction. The Soviet delegate, Andrei Vishinsky, said that the Western plan had kept him awake most of the night laughing. Of course, the Soviet order of priorities was the exact opposite of the Western ranking.

The occurrence of a number of momentous events at this time opened the way to a lessening of tension between East and West. The Korean War had ground to a stalemate; Premier Stalin had died in the Kremlin; the unbelievably generous Austrian State Treaty had been signed by the Soviet Union; and the heads of state had met at the summit in Geneva.

The Disarmament Committee, on April 23, 1954, set up a subcommittee of five consisting of the Soviet Union, the United States, the United Kingdom, France and Canada. Britain and France submitted a memorandum of disarmament objectives in May 1954 proposing a reduction in armed forces to one million each for the Soviet Union, China, and the United States and 800,000 for Britain and France; abolition of weapons of mass destruction; and phased reduction of conventional arms, all under inspection control. In the first stage of the disarmament treaty, there was to be a simple freeze of conventional forces. This was to be followed in the second stage by 50 per cent of the projected conventional cut, accompanied by a cut-off in the production of fissionable material for use in nuclear weapons. Not until the third stage were nuclear stockpiles to be destroyed, and then only after the remaining 50 per cent of the conventional cut-off had been achieved.

The Soviets at first rejected the Anglo-French proposals out of hand, calling instead for an immediate ban on nuclear weapons and the familiar one-third across the board reduction in conventional forces. Later in 1954, the Russians relented somewhat and agreed to accept the Anglo-French proposals as a basis for discussion.

In March 1955 the Western powers proffered some concessions. They offered to destroy the nuclear weapons somewhat earlier, that is, halfway through stage three, after 75 per cent of the conventional forces had been disbanded. Further, the West offered new force levels so that the three major powers would be allowed 1.5 million men each and Great Britain and France 650,000 each.

The stage was set for the Soviet delegate, Jacob Malik, to astound the subcommittee and the world on May 10, 1955, by submitting a draft declaration that in effect accepted the terms of the British-French memorandum. He even agreed to inspectors who "within the limits of the control function they exercise would have unhindered access at any time to all objects of control."

Philip Noel-Baker called this date "the moment of hope." The French delegate Jules Moch exulted, "I would say that the whole thing looks too good to be true . . . practically all of our proposals accepted." The American delegate, Harold Stassen, President Eisenhower's Special Assistant on Disarmament, was carried away with the vision of the success of his mission.

Any reader of this book could have predicted the outcome of this "moment of hope." The second act had to be what has been termed the "Western volte face of 1955." Only a week earlier, on May 3, 1955, the American delegate had prodded the Soviets. He declared, "Fifteen days have elapsed since the Franco-British proposal" and went on to state that if an answer was not forthcoming promptly, he could "arrive at no conclusion than that there is no desire to negotiate." Now, Harold Stassen was recalled for consultation.

He reappeared before the subcommittee 111 days later, on August 29, 1955, with the following statement: "The United States does now place a reservation upon all its pre-Geneva substantive positions taken in this subcommittee or in the disarmament committee or in the United Nations." Mr. Stassen startled the delegates both of the Western Allies and the Soviet Union by backing away from all previous American proposals except for the open skies idea which President Eisenhower had mentioned at the Geneva Summit on July 21, 1955.

Mr. Stassen later explained the American position: "It is the United States view that low levels and drastic reduction in armaments—even though carried out under an armaments agreement—would not, if they were not accompanied by progress in the settlement of major political issues, be in the interest of any country represented at this Subcommittee table. These reductions would increase the danger of the outbreak of war at some point in the world." This is certainly the queerest logic—and sheerest double-talk—ever to emanate from the mouth of the head of a major delgation to a major disarmament conference. One wonders what on earth the delegates were doing at the Subcommittee table in the first place. It is interesting to note that the Soviet Union had previously attempted to correlate the stages of disarmament to the settlement of political issues but that the United States had rejected this position as preposterous.

The Subcommittee dragged on for 157 meetings until the Soviet Union refused, on October 28, 1957, to participate any further. Varying ceilings on armed forces were proposed; there was talk of outer space control, of a ban on testing of atomic weapons, of open skies, of a proposed cutoff of future atomic weapons, of international control of guided rockets. All came to nothing. The United States insisted that its disarmament package was inseparable and had to be accepted on an all or nothing basis.

Philip Noel-Baker juxtaposed the proposals of the Soviet Union and the Western governments in 1957 and concluded, "On paper the Russians were offering to accept much more disarmament and much more inspection and control than the West." Sayville R. Davis, writing in the Fall, 1960, issue of *Daedalus*, echoed the same viewpoint: "For several critical years, the habit of pretending to work for disarmament served to mask the fact that the political leadership of the United States did not want disarmament."

It might be stated, as a general observation, that the United States, before or since 1957, has never defined its disarmament position with any precision. American proposals only seem to apply to first steps—first steps to what?

A Surprise Attack Conference was held in Geneva from

October to December, 1958. Since the American U-2's were already photographing every square inch of Soviet territory, it is puzzling to try to understand why President Eisenhower offered his open skies proposal. Perhaps he wanted to legitimatize the activity. The Russians offered to open the skies over the Siberian tundras. The Americans didn't much care because a tour of the Woolworth stores would have yielded postcards blanketing the country. The outcome here was another fat zero.

In search of a forum to continue the quest for disarmament, the 1958 General Assembly turned back to the United Nations Disarmament Commission, which was enlarged to include all eighty-two members. The foreign ministers of the four major powers met in Geneva in August 1959 and decided to make a new effort towards general disarmament. This took the form of a ten-nation disarmament committee composed of five NATO and five Warsaw power representatives to which the Commission delegated the actual work on September 7, 1959. The Russians had resolved never again to be outnumbered on such committees.

The Ten-Power Conference convened on March 15, 1960, and dragged on until June 27, 1960, when the Soviet bloc representatives abruptly walked out to the cries by Jules Moch of "scandale," probably as a result of the fiasco of the May 1960 summit meeting in Paris. Discussion of general disarmament was not to be resumed until March 1962 when the eighteen-nation Geneva committee, which had been set up outside of the United Nations framework as a result of bilateral Soviet-American talks, convened.

All this time, explosions of atomic and thermonuclear test bombs were sweeping up into the atmosphere ever increasing quantities of materials made radioactive by neutrons. As the gases in the fireball cooled, solid dust particles were formed, which were carried around the world by winds, to be deposited by rain and snow. This radioactive fallout could not be seen, felt, tasted, smelled or heard as it drifted gently and softly onto the fields, meadows and waters below to be accumulated finally in the human bones and glands.

John Foster Dulles insisted that tests were necessary to develop smaller, cleaner weapons. One cannot resist quoting Norman Cousins in this regard: "Almost without realizing it, we are adopting the language of madmen. We talk of clean hydrogen bombs as though we are dealing with the ultimate in moral refinement. We use fairyland words to describe a mechanism that in the split second can incinerate millions of human beings . . . to call a hydrogen bomb or any bomb clean is to make an obscene farce of words."

The Soviet physicist Professor A. M. Kuzin published an article in mid-1958 estimating that if nuclear tests were continued, "then the price paid by future generations will roughly be at the rate of 7,000,000 lives per generation, due to various diseases caused by the appearance in the atmosphere of radioactive products of nuclear explosions." Dr. Linus Pauling warned "that the pool of human germ plasm, which determines the nature of the human race, is deteriorating." The French biologist Jean Rostand called continuation of the tests *le crime dans l'avenir*—the crime projected into the future. A great outcry arose against the testing that was befouling the planetary environment and threatening to make the planet uninhabitable.

The first political demand for a halt to atmospheric tests had been made by the then Indian Prime Minister Jawaharlal Nehru on April 2, 1954. The Soviet Union had suggested a two- to three-year ban on tests, with inspection, in June, 1957. After completing a long series of tests, which dumped a great deal of fallout, the Russians announced a unilateral suspension of testing in March, 1958. A conference of experts on detection of nuclear tests during a proposed period of suspension convened in Geneva on July 1, 1958. By August 21, 1958, the scientists, from both sides of the Iron Curtain, had agreed on the technical fundamentals.

Thereupon, representatives of the Soviet Union, the United Kingdom, and the United States met October 31, 1958, at Geneva for the Conference on the Discontinuance of Nuclear Weapons Tests. The next month each of the three powers announced an unofficial, unpoliced moratorium on testing. Until that time the United States had conducted explosions with a total force of 130 megatons, the Soviet Union of 50 megatons.

The calm was not disturbed until France exploded its first atomic bomb in the Sahara on February 13, 1960. That country conducted two more tests that year and another in April 1961. The larger powers had extended the test moratorium from year to year, conditioned upon the others not resuming testing. Then, after having clandestinely prepared for new tests while pretending to negotiate their cessation at Geneva, the Soviets resumed atmospheric testing on September 1, 1961, with a series including the largest explosion in history—with an energy of fifty-eight megatons.

At first, the United States retaliated only with underground tests in Nevada. But, after assessing the Soviet test program, the United States decided that it, too, would have to resume atmospheric testing in order to keep abreast in the race towards annihilation. The result was a marked increase in the concentration of Strontium 90, Iodine 131, Carbon 14 and Cesium 137 absorbed by the plants that are eaten by food animals. Thus radioactivity was incorporated into the animals' flesh and milk. The United States, Britain, Sweden, Canada, Austria, and other countries considered the halting of fresh milk supplies to children.

The ill feeling resulting from the violation of the test moratorium terminated the Geneva conference on discontinuance of testing on January 29, 1962, after 353 sessions. But an aroused world refused to accept this defeat. Picketing, demonstrations, marches, protests, and sit-ins agitated for the end to the war on babies. By unanimous vote, the General Assembly of the United Nations called on the nuclear powers to end all nuclear weapons testing by January 1, 1963.

This deadline was not met, but during the summer of 1963, at Moscow, there was negotiated another partial success in the long history of disarmament. This was the test ban treaty, which was signed by the United States, Britain, and the Soviet Union on August 5, 1963. (France and the People's Republic of China refused to sign.) The treaty was a limited one, banning weapon tests in the atmosphere, in outer space and under water. The treaty did not provide for the reduction of nuclear stockpiles nor halt the continued production of nuclear weapons nor restrict their use in time of war.

Because the countries could not agree on the number

of on-site inspections, and because the United States claimed that such tests could be detected only by detection monitor stations on Soviet soil, underground testing was omitted from the ban. In fact, however, the United States had secretly concealed that it had been monitoring such tests since February 2, 1962, through its LASA (Large Aperture Seismic Array), when it had detected seismic signals from the Soviet nuclear weapons proving ground in the Semipalatensk area of Central Asia.

Nevertheless, President Kennedy was fully justified in addressing the American people in a new "spirit of hope" and in hailing the treaty as a "shaft of light cut into the darkness."

Unfortunately, however, the process of ratification just about snuffed out this shaft of light. The treaty was argued before the Senate, not from the noblest, but from the narrowest of motives. Secretary McNamara defended the treaty as a "prolongation of our technological superiority." One searches, almost in vain, the record of Senate committee testimony for a sense of humanitarian responsibility to the children of Utah, Nevada, Japan and elsewhere and to the yet unborn who will suffer cancer, leukemia, stillbirths and other defects; for a decent concern for the alarm of the rest of mankind that the atmosphere would be befouled and the earth rendered uninhabitable. Instead, the peoples of the earth were appalled and horrified at the image of an America sick with fear and anxiety lest its stockpile of tens of thousands of nuclear warheads and its overkill capacity to destroy the Soviet Union 1,250 times be inadequate for security.

The *New York Times* commented editorially, "The nuclear test-ban treaty is coming into the world like an unwanted child. . . . The great sense of relief that went round the world when the treaty was first initialed is being attacked as simple-minded and unrealistic. It is hard to believe that this is the same treaty signed with such high drama in Moscow by the Foreign Ministers and endorsed by dozens of countries all over the globe. . . . A treaty smothered in a blanket of fear and distrust represents a poor foundation for further progress."

What more eloquent testimony is required than the fact that the United States Senate voted the largest defense budget in peacetime history by a vote of 77 to 0 on the afternoon of the same day (September 24, 1963) on which the test ban treaty was ratified 80 to 19.

Why did the United States and the Soviet Union sign the limited test ban treaty? For years, the two giant nuclear powers, making separate calculations of the military balance, alternately favored and resisted a test ban under different conditions at different times. Were the two giants proffering a sop to alarmed public opinion? Was the United States seeking to retard Soviet progress while prolonging its own lead? Did the Soviet Union figure that an 145 overkill capacity was enough? Was Khrushchev stealing a march on the Chinese communists? Or did the Russians hope to curry favor with the Asian, African and uncommitted nations? It is reported that Marshall Rodion Y. Malinovsky and the Soviet chiefs of staff opposed the test ban.

The tenor of the hearings before the Senate Foreign Relations Committee was a harbinger of things to come under the limited test ban treaty. As a condition for their support of the treaty, the military chiefs and the Congress had exacted certain "safeguards" from the executive branch. These included a commitment that the United States would continue to carry out an aggressive test program.

As we noted above, because of differences over inspection requirements, the treaty contained one loophole permitting underground tests. At the time, it was presumed that severe restraints had been imposed upon future testing because of the technical difficulties and costs of conducting underground tests. However, both sides have been able to get around the apparent restraints by drilling deeper and devising more sophisticated instrumentation.

The result is that both sides have been steadily increasing the size (to the force of over one megaton) and number of their underground tests. They have also been able to acquire much of the diagnostic information on weapons design and effects that once could be obtained only through atmospheric tests.

Thus, it could be reported, on November 30, 1967, that the United States Atomic Energy Commission was making unexpectedly rapid progress in developing radically new atomic weapons in the accelerating arms race as a result of underground testing in Nevada. Another brittle treaty is laid to rest.

On October 17, 1963, the United Nations Assembly unanimously approved a resolution prohibiting nuclear arms or other weapons of mass destruction in space. An agreement embodying this concept had previously been reached by the Soviet Union and the United States. Although this agreement, in itself, had little practical value at the moment, it was believed to be of psychological value at a time when the world was looking for some further step after the Moscow treaty.

The space resolution was put in treaty form by the United Nations Committee on the Peaceful Uses of Outer Space. It was approved unanimously by the General Assembly on December 19, 1966, and signed by the United States, the Soviet Union, and sixty other countries on January 27, 1967.

It was to be anticipated, of course, that, in the hearings on the treaty, the Joint Chiefs of Staff would give their endorsement only on the condition that ratification would lead to increased (not decreased) United States military activity in space.

Unfortunately, the treaty on the peaceful uses of space has not moved any closer that day when American and Soviet astronauts "will meet on the moon as brothers." We have already discussed above how the gaping loopholes in this accord are being exploited by the military technologists of both sides. Incidentally, although the United Nations established a Committee on Outer Space in 1958 and has drafted a treaty on the subject, there has yet been no agreement on the definition of the term "outer space."

"You'll get pie in the sky when you die—that's a lie."

In the interim, the task of going forward had been passed back to what had become the seventeen-nation Geneva conference (France had never occupied her two empty seats at the conference table). Since March 14, 1962, the negotiations had dragged on with the West represented by the United States, Britain, Italy and Canada; the Warsaw powers by the Soviet Union, Poland, Rumania, Bulgaria and Czechoslovakia; and the neutral nations by Brazil, Burma, Ethiopia, India, Mexico, Nigeria, the United Arab Republic and Sweden.

The promise of hope for these negotiations was particularly strong because the sessions had been preceded by an agreed statement of principles by the Soviet Union and the United States that set forth the fundamentals for disarmament. The Joint Statement of Agreed Principles for Disarmament Negotiations of September 20, 1961, had been formulated by the McCloy-Zorin negotiations.

The Joint Statement read as follows: "Noting with concern that the continuing arms race is a heavy burden for humanity and is fraught with dangers for the cause of world peace, the goal of negotiation is to achieve agreement on a program which will ensure that disarmament is general and complete and war is no longer an instrument for settling international problems . . . that states will have at their disposal only those non-nuclear armaments as are agreed to be necessary to maintain internal order . . . that weapons are to be disbanded and discontinued by balanced stages within specified time limits."

The statement concluded: "All disarmament measures should be implemented from beginning to end under such strict and effective international control as would provide firm assurance that all parties are honoring their obligations. . . . An International Disarmament Organization should be created within the framework of the United Nations . . . its inspectors should be assured unrestricted access without veto to all places as necessary for the purpose of effective verification."

The naïve or unenlightened observer might have believed that the long-sought-for millennium had finally arrived. But the reader of this book should know better by now. He would not have to be a prophet to predict that the probable course of the seventeen-nation conference would be another exercise in utter futility. For the first fruit of hope of the test ban to have been followed by a larger harvest would have contradicted the whole history of disarmament negotiation.

Since the Soviet Union was deficient in nuclear missiles, it proposed their destruction within eighteen months in the first stage of disarmament. The United States objected that this step would leave the Soviet Union with a great advantage because of its powerful conventional forces. The Soviet Union then offered, on September 19, 1963, as a concession, a nuclear umbrella whereby the two great nuclear powers would each retain, on their own territory, a limited number of missiles, not submarine based, for protective purposes. The United States, fearing that these proposals would tip the balance of power and alter the mix of armaments in Moscow's favor, came back with a demand for across-the-board cuts of 30 per cent in the first and 35 per cent in each of the next stages for all major arms categories.

The Soviet Union revived the 1957 Rapacki plan for a central European zone free of nuclear weapons. This idea was questioned by the West on the grounds that it would remove the protection of defensive nuclear missiles from countries facing the great mass of Soviet ground and air forces.

Aware of the American superiority in this field, President Johnson proposed, on January 21, 1964, a verified freeze on the number of strategic nuclear delivery vehicles. This suggestion was coupled with a demand for international control of all delivery vehicles, mainly long-range bombers and missiles, at the disposal of the countries, and also over the production of these vehicles. Soviet Foreign Minister Andrei A. Gromyko pointed out that the United States was seeking "to establish international control over the most secret weapons and the most secret types of military production" without disarmament. The whole freeze proposal was dismissed as "propaganda."

The United States proposed a "bonfire" by both sides of obsolescent bombers whereby she would destroy in a two year period, 480 B-47 bombers in exchange for an equal number of TU-16's. Mr. Gromyko dismissed this as "not useful in the least." He added that "every soldier knows full well that one obsolescent bomber can be replaced by another more modern one." Mr. Gromyko might also have noted that the United States was coincidentally replacing its bombers with intercontinental ballistic missiles.

Then the Americans came forward with a demand for a halt in the production of fissionable materials for nuclear bombs. That was understandable because the United States had so much enriched Uranium and Plutonium around, it didn't know where to store the stuff. It was estimated that the surplus of ore stocks amounted to over $1 billion and was sufficient to carry bomb production into the late 1970's. But the Russian inventory was not that plentiful at that time so nothing came of this proposal either. At a later date, however, on April 20, 1964, when Soviet reactor production of Uranium-235 had caught up with demand, President Johnson and Chairman Khrushchev announced mutual reductions in Plutonium production.

The Soviets insisted on priority for their proposal to cut defense budgets by 10 to 15 per cent. But the West objected that no one even knew what the budgets were for the Iron Curtain countries and that such an idea would require verification. Of course, this could not be.

The West wanted to post observers on both sides of the Curtain to warn of surprise attacks. The Russians agreed that was a good idea and then went on to say that the number of foreign troops in Germany could, therefore, be reduced. The West rejected the link.

Of course, the Soviets, not having foreign bases, wanted to have disarmament begin with the elimination of these bases and the evacuation of all troops from abroad. It followed that the West, which had ringed Soviet territory with its installations, did not take too kindly to this idea.

So it went, down the list of measures proposed by one side or the other. The United States reiterated its position that the "radical reduction" in strategic arms demanded by Moscow at an early stage would be "decidedly in Russia's favor" and "would upset the present balance and create more danger than it eliminated." The Soviets insisted that Washington's plan for gradual cuts by agreed percentages was "unrealistic" and designed to maintain the existing balance of power between the two sides until the completion of disarmament. The seventeen-nation conference adjourned on September 17, 1964, and the Soviet delegate, Semyon K. Tsarapkin, summed up the barren accomplishments of the negotiations to that point—a "gloomy and depressing figure of zero."

For months after that adjournment, Washington and London tried, in vain, to get Moscow to agree to a resumption of the disarmament talks. Finally and unexpectedly, the Soviet Union, on March 31, 1965, asked the Secretary General to reconvene the United Nations Disarmament

Commission, which had not met since August, 1960. Because the Soviet bloc and the West could not agree on which states to include or leave out, this Commission had grown, in the interim, to include all 114 members of the United Nations.

The unwieldy size of the Commission, which began its sessions on April 21, 1965, lent itself more to polemics than to achievements. Indeed, a good part of the debate was consumed by strident attacks on United States foreign policy from Cuba to the Congo to Vietnam. However, the Commission did adopt a resolution, 89 to 0, with 16 abstentions (including the United States), recommending that the twentieth General Assembly give urgent consideration to convening a world disarmament conference to which Red China and Indonesia would be invited. Another resolution, approved 83 to 1 with 18 abstentions (including the Soviet bloc and France), called for an early resumption of intensive negotiations by the seventeen-nation Geneva disarmament conference. The Commission wound up its work on June 16, 1965.

After a lapse of ten months, the seventeen-nation conference resumed at the Palais des Nations on July 27, 1965. Britain's Lord Chalfont stated, "This summer in Geneva may be our last chance. I hope that we shall not let it pass." A message from President Johnson declared, "If we love man, nothing is more important than the effort to diminish danger—halt the spread of nuclear power—and bring the weapons of war under increasing control." He termed this "as the most important task on earth."

Uppermost in the minds of the delegates was the need to stop the spread of nuclear weapons. As long ago as 1961, the General Assembly had urged unanimously that nuclear weapons not be produced by, nor transferred to, non-nuclear nations. To this end, the United States, on August 17, 1965, submitted a draft for an atom arms pact. But, here again, the United States came forward with unclean hands in the same way that Bernard Baruch had twenty years earlier.

V. C. Trivedi, the delegate from India, best summarized these objections. He said that India refused to accept the "unrealistic and irrational proposition that a non-proliferation treaty should impose obligations only on non-nuclear powers while the nuclear powers continued to hold on to their privileged status or club membership by retaining and even increasing their deadly stockpiles." Shades of E. M. Forster, sahib Johnson.

In a similar vein, Franz Josef Strauss, former West German Defense Minister, writing in the *Rheinsiche Merkur* of Cologne, decried the attempt to disarm the potential nuclear weapons "owners of tomorrow" while the present nuclear powers preserved their monopoly. He further warned that if Germany was subjected to "military discrimination," as in the Treaty of Versailles, a new Führer might emerge who "would promise and probably also acquire nuclear weapons."

Senator Robert F. Kennedy said on the floor of the United States Senate, "The most vital issue now facing the nation and the world . . . is not Vietnam or the Dominican Republic or Berlin. It is the question of nuclear proliferation—of the mounting threat posed by the spread of nuclear weapons." Prime Minister Harold Wilson echoed these sentiments. He declared, "If in 1966 we do not succeed in negotiating an effective and watertight treaty to stop the spread of nuclear weapons, the world may have passed the point of no return."

Unfortunately, in what has been called the *n*th-plus-one-country problem, each nuclear power clutches tightly to its own bosom its atomic playthings while believing that the big problem is to stop that next country after itself from acquiring the same toys. Each nuclear power loudly proclaims the sheer logic of the postion that thermonuclear bombs are harmless in its own possession but devastatingly dangerous when held by the next power.

Thus, in submitting a draft treaty that allowed for a NATO multi-lateral nuclear force, Mr. Johnson must have had his tongue in his cheek. He knew that the Soviet Union would never countenance such a loophole. In fact, the American proposal was not even fully acceptable to the other three Western powers represented at Geneva, although it had been characterized as "the product of close collaboration among the NATO countries represented here." A *New York Times* editorial called the whole thing the "debacle at Geneva." It came as no surprise, then, when the Soviets rejected the American draft as a "joke," a cynical attempt to admit West Germany to the nuclear club by the back door.

It would seem that many of the neutral nations also opposed the American position. For example, Mrs. Alva Myrdal, the Swedish delegate, stated that the question of nuclear sharing among the NATO powers was an "obstacle for truly responsible negotiations."

To close this loophole, the United States later offered an amended draft to define control as the "right or ability to fire nuclear weapons without the concurrent decision of an existing nuclear weapons state." It was argued that such a veto means that "no additional state and no association of states gains the right or ability to make, on its own, a decision to use nuclear weapons." The Russian reaction was that the amended draft "changed nothing," still left a "gaping loophole," and had not advanced the negotiations "one inch."

The whole question of non-proliferation is puzzling to the observer. Here is one case where the smaller powers can really accomplish something on their own. Instead of blaming the big powers, instead of waiting while the nuclear nations haggle, why don't the non-nuclear countries act on their own initiative? The smaller nations have it within their power to halt proliferation without further delay by simply pledging not to receive or build the bombs. Could it be that they are not really opposed to proliferation? Could it be that they agree with Indonesia that the best way to prevent nuclear war is to provide every country with atomic bombs? That is the theory of deterrence carried to its ultimate, logical end.

At the resumed session, the United Arab Republic proposed a formal extension of the limited, unverified test ban to underground explosions above the threshold of 4.75 on the seismic scale, roughly the size of the Hiroshima bomb. A voluntary moratorium would be placed on smaller tests. While the Soviet delegate, Semyon K. Tsarapkin, declared Moscow would sign such a pact "without delay," the United States representative, William C. Foster, turned down the suggestion as of "no interest" on the familiar grounds that the plan lacked provisions for on-site inspections to prevent cheating. The latter declared, "half-way measures may create suspicions." It might be noted that a completely unverified ban on underground testing is a retreat from the former Soviet position that would have allowed three on-site inspections annually.

The 1965 sessions of the seventeen-nation disarmament conference recessed on September 16, 1965, with East and West each blaming the other for failure to reach any new arms-control agreements. Mr. Foster best characterized the work of the session as "exhibitions of poisonous polemics."

The twentieth General Assembly, on November 19, 1965, by a 93 to 0 vote urged "all states to take all steps necessary for the early conclusion of a treaty preventing the proliferation of nuclear weapons." To that end, the Geneva committee was called upon to "reconvene as early as possible" to draft such a treaty "void of any loopholes."

On November 29, 1965, the General Assembly adopted 112 to 0, with France abstaining and Nationalist China not participating, a resolution urging that steps be taken for the convening "of a world disarmament conference not later than 1967." The Chinese Communist Foreign Ministry promptly announced that Peking "will certainly not take part" in such a world disarmament conference.

After the adjournment of the twentieth session, Secretary-General U Thant assessed its work by declaring that "the earlier promise of a genuine relaxation of tensions among nations seemed to have faded away."

The eyes of the world turned back to Geneva where the seventeen-nation disarmament conference resumed on January 27, 1966.

The United States proposed that each of the two giant powers destroy "thousands" of their nuclear weapons in order that an agreed-upon amount of Uranium 235 might be transferred to peaceful purposes. The United States had offered to transfer 60,000 kilograms of this material if the Soviet Union provided 40,000 kilograms. Here again, it must be remembered that the United States has many, many more bombs than Russia and that it consequently must have a tremendous store of obsolete bombs because it started making them so much earlier. This plan may be likened to the bomber bonfire which had been previously proposed. The Soviet delegate, Mr. Tsarapkin, rightly commented that this proposal has "nothing in common with disarmament, nor does it reduce the nuclear danger."

Instead, Mr. Tsarapkin again came forth with a demand for a ban on underground nuclear tests, but without inspection, and for the removal of all troops from foreign territories. The American delegate, Adrian Fisher, rejoined with the standard reply that withdrawal of troops "would impair the right of collective self-defense permitted under the United Nations Charter."

Another seven months of "useless word-mongering" followed before the 1966 sessions were recessed on August 25. The anti-proliferation treaty made no progress despite President Johnson's plea for "compromise language which we can both live with."

The United Nations General Assembly voted the annual appeal for completion of a treaty to halt the spread of nuclear armaments on November 4, 1966. This time the text called for a "balance" of obligations of both nuclear and non-nuclear states.

A hopeful turn came when the two sides shifted their negotiations, in October, 1966, from Geneva to private discussions between Soviet Foreign Minister Gromyko, President Johnson and Secretary of State Rusk. Perhaps spurred by the common threat of Chinese militancy, the United States and the Soviet Union finally recognized that here was one case where their interests were identical. Alphonse and Gaston discovered they were on the same side of the charade.

History repeats itself. In 1946, the United States sought to make permanent its temporary nuclear monopoly through the Acheson-Baruch-Lilienthal Plan. In 1967, the United States and the Soviet Union sought to perpetuate and crystallize in treaty form their practical nuclear monopoly. They sought to ban the spread of nuclear weapons to countries that did not yet possess them while leaving themselves free to improve and multiply their own arsenals.

In taking this action, the Soviets have cast themselves completely adrift from their erstwhile Chinese allies while the United States has abandoned its so-called NATO allies to the status of Russian hostages. The proposed multi-lateral nuclear force, of course, had to be scrapped as part of the bargain.

Atomic Confederacy thus overrode the sovereign rights of the former associates in NATO, the Warsaw Pact and the uncommitted bloc and froze them into a position of permanent dependence and subservience. Their second-class status is thus institutionalized by treaty. The two major powers, in brushing aside the appeal for a balance of obligations, imposed an inequality of sacrifice. The end result is a formal system of two classes of nations, the haves and the have-nots, and those who now have are not committed to any meaningful reciprocal gestures of any kind.

Felix von Eckardt, a Christian Democratic member of the West German Bundestag, summarized the proposition, as follows: "Nonproliferation is like a club of notorious

boozers who demand a written agreement from the teetotalers that they never take alcohol and won't even touch
a drop when a glass is offered them. And then after the
pact is signed, these drinkers not only sit together and
booze it up again, but also throw the empty bottles at
the teetotalers."

The seventeen nation disarmament conference recon-
vened in Geneva on February 21, 1967. On August 24,
the United States and the Soviet Union submitted separate, but identical, texts of a draft treaty to prevent the
further spread of nuclear weapons. Each draft left blank
Article III on inspection. This blank was later filled in,
on January 18, 1968, when both major powers yielded to
the objections of West Germany and permitted Euratom
to continue its inspection system subject to certification
within two years by the International Atomic Energy
Agency.

Despite pledges given by the United States, the Soviet
Union and Britain for the protection, through the Security
Council, of non-nuclear signatories against nuclear attack,
the draft treaty had to be offered to the General Assem-
bly, on April 24, 1968, without the formal approval of the
Geneva disarmament conference.

Again, the age old law of the jungle prevailed and the
weak nations put aside their reservations and submitted
to the will of the superpowers. The non-nuclear countries
swallowed the bitter pill of self-renunciation on June 12,
1968 when the United Nations General Assembly approved the anti-proliferation treaty by a vote of 95 to 4,
with 21 abstentions. France and Red China again did
not sign.

Despite the pledge by President Johnson of prompt

ratification of what he termed, "the most important international agreement in the field of disarmament since the nuclear age began," some doubt has been cast on the final ratification of the treaty. The Russian invasion of Czechoslovakia and the American Presidential election have opened new strains in their Atomic Confederacy. The readers of this book have witnessed the snuffing out of too many other "moments of hope."

What does the anti-proliferation treaty have to do with disarmament? The answer here again is: absolutely nothing. Not a single atomic weapon—strategic or tactical—will be defused or scrapped as a result of this treaty. Neither the United States nor the Soviet Union will pause for an instant in the course of their newly accelerated arms race.

That is a pity, for one would imagine that halting the spread of nuclear weapons would interlock and be interdependent with the banning of underground nuclear tests and the suspension of nuclear weapon production. True, the preamble to the treaty declares the intention of the two governments "to achieve at the earliest possible date the cessation of the nuclear arms race." But barely one month after submitting this declaration, the United States announced a new armaments program that both the Kennedy and Johnson administrations had previously resisted for fear of further expanding the arms race with the Soviet Union.

History has witnessed many attempts to disarm involuntarily a temporarily secondary nation. The treaties of Versailles and Brest-Litovsk are good examples. Invariably, these treaties cannot endure under the nation-state system. Even if an existing government is willing to sign a blank check on the future of its country, a future stronger government will repudiate the signature. Whether clandestinely or openly, such a treaty will be violated.

So, despite the actions taken at Moscow, the United Nations and Geneva, the citizen must still raise his voice and call for disarmament. In the words of President Johnson, "The time is now, the hour is late. The fate of generations yet unborn is in our hands." The United States Arms Control and Disarmament Agency may declare, "that, in complicated and politically sensitive arms control and disarmament negotiations, a year of unrealized initiatives does not mean failure." No, it may mean death. Entirely too many years of "unrealized initiatives" have gone by. Time is running out.

Nor does Secretary-General U Thant agree with the American agency. He states, "Time is running short and every day's delay entails untold risks. The greatest risk lies in doing nothing, in wasting time, in hair-splitting, and meanwhile piling up nuclear and thermonuclear weapons."

How much longer must the world continue to witness what Robert Hutchins called, "the repellant spectacle of governments proclaiming peace while they arm to the teeth."

9

The Why of Disarmament
Negotiation

The small first steps represented by the test ban, space
and anti-proliferation treaties have not been "the start
of a long and fruitful journey" toward disarmament. These
first sprouts of international confidence have not flowered.
The reader of this book will not share the general gloom
and disappointment that have followed the failure to
exploit the favorable opportunities that presented themselves after the signing of these treaties.

He will understand that the treaties were completely
inconsequential in their impact on great world issues because they, like the hot line and the agreement to return
fallen astronauts, were completely marginal and periph-
eral to the central problem of disarmament. The treaties
may have served biological, psychological or humanitarian
purposes. They may have temporarily calmed the fears
of millions of people. But they had nothing to do with

disarmament because they did not cause the destruction of a single nuclear weapon nor did they halt, for even one second, the production of new atomic bombs.

The tipoff is that not one of these treaties was adopted over the protests of the military. They consented, in each case, either because the possibilities of the outlawed procedures had already been exhausted or because they were promised even further opportunities for expansion. Such treaties must be suspect.

Never perhaps in the relations between nations has any policy been so universally professed and espoused as has the policy of disarmament in recent years. Never has any policy been the subject of so much discussion and negotiation between nations. Never has such extended negotiations yielded so little progress. Never has failure in the relations between nations been so absolute and complete.

The marathon of disarmament negotiation cannot point to even one tiny, innocuous weapon that has been scrapped —not one slingshot, one cap pistol, one bomb. The diplomats could not even agree on fundamental definitions, such as, what is peace, or what is aggression, or what is China, or what is a weapon—or, for that matter, what is disarmament. In the words of President Kennedy, "Disarmament remains a pious phrase which both sides invoke—but which they will not invoke together."

The citizen cannot conceive how it was possible for the greatest talents of our democracy to address themselves so unstintingly, for so long a period, to the question of disarmament without the slightest result. Certainly, any business would long ago have turned out a board of directors with such a record of utter failure. Can it be that so much time, energy, effort and talent have been expended in sheer fakery, to hoodwink the peoples of the world? The citizen instinctively rejects that suggestion. Yet we have the word of Anthony Nutting, who participated in many disarmament conferences: "I cannot honestly say that I believe there was ever a moment in all these negotiations when a real agreement was a practical possibility."

Then why do these disarmament conferences meet? Why are the representatives of the nations of the world negotiating at this very moment concerning disarmament?

We have here put our finger on the very crux of the subject of disarmament. If we can analyze the motivation that drives nations to negotiate, without end, in a search for disarmament; if, once we have gathered the plenipotentiaries around the conference table, we can provide the reasons for the abject failure of the negotiations to this point, then we might try to build some structure of hope on the rubble and ruins of the past. Otherwise, this volume has degenerated into another chronicle of the failures of disarmament negotiations—another in the dozens of books that gather dust on the library shelves. Unless this book strikes the mainspring that gives life to these disarmament conferences, these pages will have served no purpose and have no reason for being.

The voices cry, "Each day we draw nearer the hour of maximum danger"; "with each swing of the pendulum the time to save civilization grows shorter." They demand, with Pope Paul VI, "It is necessary to negotiate, to negotiate without tiring." They declare, with President Kennedy, "Let us begin anew—remembering on both sides that civility is not a sign of weakness and sincerity is always subject to proof. Let us never negotiate out of fear. But let us never fear to negotiate."

The diplomats are reminded that the quest for disarmament is not "a sign of weakness." They are consoled that they do not have to love their enemies to talk with them, that an agreement is not a compact with the devil, that a reciprocal concession is not a surrender to absolute evil. They are warned that "to close the door to the conference room is to open a door to war."

With all due respect, it is difficult to understand these frantic calls for negotiation because the record will show that there has been almost continuous negotiation on disarmament since the end of World War II. Representatives of the West and of the Soviet bloc have met for hundreds upon hundreds of sessions and they have bargained hard and conscientiously and diligently.

Nor does it square with the facts to accuse the diplomats of paying only lip service to the idea of disarmament; of simply going through the motions of negotiations without any serious intent, upon their part, to succeed. One wonders whether those who charge that negotiations are more and more conducted for the sake of appearances understand what is taking place.

The diplomats are meeting. They are driving ahead with all their skills and all their energies to accomplish their objectives and their assignments. It would seem that the important thing for the observer is to determine exactly what the diplomats are negotiating. In order to understand the history of disarmament conferences, the citizen must address his inquiries to the nature of the objectives and assignments given to the plenipotentiaries.

Review the history of disarmament negotiations as related in the two preceding chapters. You must conclude, beyond cavil, that the diplomats were trying diligently to achieve disarmament—disarmament of the other side. That is why so much of the negotiations seem to take on the air of an Alphonse-Gaston harlequinade. "You, the United States, have overseas bases, therefore, we will eliminate them first." "You, the Soviet Union, have bigger armies, so we will begin by cutting them drastically." "You, Uncle Sam, lead in Polaris missiles, therefore, they should be outlawed immediately." "You, Ivan, have a closed society so let us make a start by instituting inspection procedures." "You, nonnuclear countries, do not have atomic weapons, so let's adopt an anti-proliferation treaty."

The tendency is to generate false hopes by enlarging in one's mind the policy-making scope and authority of the diplomats to forge agreements. This is wishful thinking. For one forgets that the diplomats are only representatives of the governments of the various nation-states and that they appear at the conference table strictly as agents. They do not represent humanity at large. When they speak or act for their countries, they do so only in accordance with precise instructions. They do not discuss the questions; they recite on them, as from a prepared script. They use the same arguments, in the same order, with the same key words. Diplomats like Cecil and Stassen deceive themselves into believing that they are bigger than their governments; they forget themselves and the realities of world organization.

The realities are that the face of the globe is divided into an absurd architecture of roughly 120 independent watertight compartments of all shapes and sizes, each a law unto itself. These compartments are called sovereign nation-states. Each state jealously admits no power or authority superior to itself. Johann Fichte correctly appraised the international situation when he stated that "between states there is neither law nor right unless it be the right of the stronger."

The guidelines set forth for princes by Nicoló Machiavelli are still scrupulously followed by all nation-states. "When the bare safety of the country is at stake no consideration of justice or injustice, of mercy or cruelty, of honor or dishonor, can find a place. Every scruple must be set aside and that plan followed which saves the country's life and preserves her liberty." The jarring, jealous, perverse nation-states, born in violence, live by violence in a continual state of war—declared or undeclared—present or potential. Militarism, war, armaments are, in reality, products and effects of the nation-state structure of the world. The business of the nation-state, as we have seen, is war and preparation for war.

And the diplomats represent this world, not some fantasy Shangri-La. To paraphrase Clausewitz, diplomacy—or political commerce—is a continuation of war, a carrying out of the same by other means. President Eisenhower has pointed out that negotiations are another way to fight a war—in effect another weapons system. One should not be shocked, therefore, to discover that disarmament negotiations are conducted mainly as psychological warfare exercises, as a means of weakening an existing or potential enemy. To quote Salvador de Madariaga, "so-called disarmament discussions are in fact armament discussions, and that, whatever the label, the commodity bought and sold in the market is power." In this sense, disarmament must be viewed, not as an isolated phenomenon, but as part of the complex of overall inter-nation-state relations.

A nation's superiority or inferiority in the power of its armaments, vis-a-vis the other side, is essentially a relative thing. Therefore, a country may actually increase its armaments relative to its adversaries while reducing them in absolute quantity. Or a nation may achieve a similar result by freezing a present temporary strategic advantage or by inhibiting the other's weapons development program.

Such being the situation, every discussion, dealing or negotiation on disarmament can, at bottom, have no other purpose than the maneuvering of the adversary into an unfavorable position. A conference on reduction of armaments is actually entered into with the deliberate intention of increasing one's own power. The diplomat's assignment is to strengthen his country's armaments by disarming, that is, by reducing his absolute position while increasing his relative arms power by means of a so-called disarmament agreement with his less astute colleagues. An objective examination of the facts can warrant no other conclusion.

In this way, disarmament negotiations themselves become a weapon in the cold war. The diplomats are like infantry scouts probing the installations of the enemy and smoking out his strengths and weaknesses. In the execution of his assignment, the diplomat utilizes all the ancient wiles of his profession. In the words of Emery Reves, "Diplomacy, like military strategy, consists of hoodwinking, tricking and outwitting the other party. . . . In every other field of human activity . . . we call this man a liar, a deceiver, a cheat." The aim is to disadvantage the enemy, separate it from its allies, cause it domestic trouble at home.

Indeed, diplomacy has been defined as the act of lying

for one's country. One cringes when one remembers Adlai Stevenson denying to the United Nations Security Council that his country was involved in the Bay of Pigs debacle. Certainly, the art of diplomacy has historically shown itself to be completely amoral and cynical.

The course of a disarmament conference unfolds like the strategy of a military campaign. Examine the disarmament proposals that have been advanced. In each, if you look closely, you will discover some hidden joker, hooker or gimmick. Small wonder, then, that past negotiations have been so hopelessly ensnarled.

Our authoritative Mr. McNamara summarizes this discussion of the whys and wherefores of disarmament negotiations. He told a Congressional committee in 1963, "My position is a very simple one on disarmament or arms control. I think we should engage in such agreements if and when, and only if and when, we can do so without reducing our power advantage. . . . I foresee no period in the future, let's say in the remaining years of this century, when we can, under today's conditions, operate without a strategic nuclear force."

Yet, according to historian Arthur M. Schlesinger, Jr., next to President Kennedy, "McNamara probably did more than any one else to sustain the disarmament drive." Mr. Schlesinger has this to say about the former Secretary of Defense: "With his sense of the horror of nuclear conflict, his understanding of the adequacy of existing stockpiles, his fear of nuclear proliferation, his analytic command of the weapons problem and his managerial instinct to do something about an irrational situation, he forever sought new ways of controlling the arms race."

But we have seen how this enlightened man buried the chances for disarmament for the balance of this century. Compare Mr. McNamara's attitude to that of Secretary of State Dean Rusk, the man who was directly responsible for disarmament negotiations. Mr. Schlesinger reports that Mr. Rusk was indifferent to the whole idea of disarmament, regarding it as "an essay in futility, if not folly."

The hollowness and sham of the diplomacy and of the military system which is supposed to save us from war thus stand exposed. Under these circumstances, how can one expect anything to materialize from the disarmament negotiations? In view of the demonstrated subservience of diplomacy to military policy, it would appear that the final nail has been driven into the coffin of disarmament.

One begins to formulate an answer to U Thant's question, "What element is lacking, so that, with all our skill and all our knowledge, we still find ourselves in the dark valley of discord and enmity? What is it that inhibits us from going forward together to enjoy the fruits of human endeavor and to reap the harvest of human experience? What (*sic*) is it that, for all our professed ideals, our hopes and our skills, peace on earth is still a distant objective, seen only dimly through the storms and turmoils of our present difficulties?"

One begins to understand why communication between nations degenerates into nothing more than an exchange of threats and why accommodation seems so impossible. One begins to understand the reasons behind President Kennedy's statement: "We are both caught up in a vicious and dangerous cycle with suspicion on one side breeding suspicion on the other." The course of disarmament negotiations shows that there is justifiable cause for this suspicion.

After one has recovered from the shock of discovery

that the negotiators are, in fact, fighting the first skirmishes of World War III and not talking about disarmament at all, one realizes that the entire subject of disarmament has been demolished. The citizen must have perceived from this recitation of the sorry story of disarmament that it is, in fact, a non-subject. There is no such thing, never has been and probably never will be. All those weighty tomes on disarmament in the library are written about a non-subject.

This writer is left in the unenviable position of having dispatched his subject in nine chapters. His predicament is not unlike that of the playwright who kills off his characters in the first act.

10

Nevertheless, Disarmament

It is related that Galileo, confronted with "irrefutable evidence" that the earth is the fixed center of the universe, stubbornly muttered, as he recanted, *"Eppure se muove"*—"nevertheless, it moves." Similarly, the citizen, confronted with irrefutable evidence that disarmament is only a mirage and a delusion, must stubbornly cling to his dream of disarmament. He has no alternative: otherwise, he is surrendering himself to the hopeless future of certain execution by incineration. With no hope of resolution of the problem of mounting armaments, man must lapse into idiotic despair.

The diplomats and the statesmen have abandoned, if they ever did hold them, any ideas of disarmament. The posture of self-righteousness, coupled with the attribution of pure evil to the other side, cancels in advance any possibility of settlement. The suspicion that every proposal by the adversary cloaks a concealed advantage means permanent stalemate. If we assume a position of

197

deadly rigidity and condemn every recognition of common interest as appeasement, we foreclose, by our *a priori* attitude, the sole alternative to war.

Nevertheless, the citizen must desperately hang on to this last chance of survival as a matter of life and death. He must make the question of disarmament his master passion, compared with which all other questions are unimportant, because the answer holds the key to his survival or extinction. There is only one item on the agenda of mankind and that item is survival of the human race.

Yet, as Norman Cousins points out, "there is far more thinking today on what is required to assure survival for a single astronaut inside a space ship, than on what is required to assure survival for the entire human species on earth." This book is not designed to preach any philosophy or creed or ideology. It does not even preach pacifism; the only ideology it advocates is survivalism.

We make only one assumption—that man wants to live. Continued armaments are incompatible with continued life. Live bombs and live people cannot coexist indefinitely. In the words of President Johnson, "uneasy is the peace that wears a nuclear crown. And we cannot be satisfied with a situation in which the world is capable of extinction in a moment of error, or madness or anger."

The appeal here is to the most selfish instincts. Therefore, the whole discussion is pitched to the lowest common human denominator—the instinct of self-preservation, the overriding desire to survive. Let us put first things first. Unless man survives, all further considerations are meaningless. Assuredly, the peoples of the earth must hold that common interest in survival which transcends national, ideological, racial, religious, economic and cultural lines.

Thus, with respect to what most of the world's people should care most about—the continuance of life—the great ideological and power struggle between the East and the West is supremely irrelevant. It is far more likely that civilization will be destroyed in a nuclear holocaust than that communism will ever become the predominant political system in the world. Life can continue only if there is peace. If there is peace and life, the hope of liberty can never be extinguished. To quote Pope Pius XII, "Nothing is lost with peace. Everything is lost with war."

We occupy this planet as temporary custodians for future generations. We have no right to squander their right to survive. To forfeit the struggle for survival is to commit a crime against the future of mankind and civilization. Certainly, it is the height of arrogance and presumption for a small segment of one generation to make the awesome decision of survival or extinction for all peoples and for all future time.

It is not claimed here that disarmament is equivalent to peace and thus to survival. President Johnson has well said, "Peace is a journey of a thousand miles and it must be taken one step at a time." Peace is not merely the absence of war; it is the presence of justice. The building of a peace with justice, under current world conditions, is a labor of generations. To quote the Preamble to the Constitution of the United Nations Economic, Social and Cultural Organization, "since wars begin in the minds of men, it is in the minds of men that the defences of peace must be constructed."

John Braine noticed a sign in the window of a Liverpool

gunsmith which expressed the idea. It read, "Guns don't kill people; people kill people." It is recognized that armaments are the reflection, and not the cause of world conflict. They are the symptoms of the unhealthy state of international life—of the fears, hostilities and tensions which threaten war. But these are the kind of symptoms from which the patient could die. Attempts to cure the world's sickness by disarmament have been compared to attempts to cure a patient by reducing the fever without attacking the cause. Professor Skobeltzyn answered that reducing the fever is often a useful thing to do.

Distinguished authorities have argued that to attempt to remove the armaments, before removing the substantive conflicts of interests, is to put the cart before the horse. David E. Lilienthal, for instance, believes that if you have peace you may achieve disarmament, but you cannot have disarmament until you have peace. Or as Bernard M. Baruch put it, "Peace does not follow disarmament, disarmament follows peace." He did not think it possible to make serious progress on disarmament until crucial political settlements were made with the Soviet Union.

It is submitted that these arguments had more validity in the era of conventional weapons. In that bygone age, the mobilization base and the industrial potential were of much more significance than the forces in being. Then, the best method to achieve peace was to remove the causes of political conflict. But, today, the forces in being are almost surely decisive. Thus, the arms themselves have become a fundamental political fact which must be faced.

It would be most dangerous, today, therefore, to wait

for such a settlement of international political problems before trying to alleviate the grave dangers of the headlong arms race and the frantic military competition. While peace is a long-term project, we live with the fact that annihilation can occur in an instant. There is no denying that the mere existence of armaments adds to the instability of peace and contributes to international tension. Vice versa, there is no denying that the existence of international political problems leads to the building up of armaments. Which of these statements is correct? They are both correct. It is the age-old question of which came first: the chicken or the egg. "Either" is the correct answer.

This happens to be a book about disarmament. But, certainly, there is no reason why a settlement of international political issues might not be strenuously pursued simultaneously with an attempt to secure a limitation of armaments. Indeed, these goals may be found to be two sides of the same coin. This two-pronged attack on the horrors of war should be pressed forward as expeditiously as is humanly possible.

Unfortunately, however, you will find that the individuals who urge us to wait with our disarmament proposals are the same ones who are most intransigent in seeking a solution of international tensions. In Vietnam, for instance, when things were going downhill, they claimed it was not the time to negotiate. When things were going better, they again said it was not the time to negotiate. That's exactly the point: for these people, it is never the right time to negotiate. For these people negotiation means surrender.

They are the ones who look only toward a military solution of existing questions. A typical spokesman for their

position, Richard M. Nixon, states, "You can only negotiate at the conference table what you can win on the
battlefield at that particular time . . . further discussion
of a negotiated settlement delays the end of the war by
simply encouraging the enemy that we are begging for
peace." They must have capitulation before there can be
peace. They are the denizens of the stiff world—the hawks.

To adopt a waiting attitude toward disarmament is to
adopt a do-nothing attitude—to throw up our hands in
despair and to abandon hope. In a world where, in the
words of ex-Prime Minister of Canada Lester B. Pearson,
"we prepare for war like precocious giants and for peace
like retarded pygmies," (the budget for the United States
Arms Control and Disarmament Agency is less than $10
million per year) a decision to postpone action on disarmament is equivalent to an imposition of a death sen-
tence on mankind and civilization. The thermonuclear
bomb has so telescoped history that it is impossible for us
to wait long years of acute danger of war while our diplomats, with their usual leisurely pace, tackle the existing
problems.

The advice to wait is an admission that the present
human dilemma is insoluble—that the only practical thing
left is to crouch upon the ground and weep. One is reminded of a great passage from Spengler: "Already the
danger is so great, for every individual, every class, every
people, that to cherish any illusion whatever is deplora-
ble. Time does not suffer itself to be halted; there is no
question of prudent retreat or wise renunciation. Only
dreamers believe that there is a way out. Optimism is
cowardice. We are born into this time and must bravely
follow the path to the destined end. There is no other

way. Our duty is to hold on to the lost position, without hope, without reserve, like the Roman soldier whose bones were found in front of a door in Pompeii, who, during the eruption of Vesuvius, died at his post because they forgot to relieve him. That is greatness."

The choice is a straightforward one—between demilitarization and annihilation. Those who reject disarmament have chosen this type of greatness—the greatness of blind death. The remaining few who refuse to abandon the slim hope of disarmament believe in the greatness of life. If it is beyond our capacity, under present world conditions, to bring about a world-wide fabric in which clashes of interest have been removed, then the only alternative is to eliminate the capacity for military action and annihilation.

Disarmament may not mean peace; it might mean survival. Disarmament is not a panacea or a cureall for all worldly ills. At best, it can only be the beginning, not the completion, of the solution of the problem of war. But it is a beginning which could enable us to move meaningfully to further steps since disarmament would foster a climate of opinion which would minimize thinking in terms of military solutions and encourage hope that international differences could be resolved by negotiation.

To those prophets of doom who cry that disarmament is a dangerous exercise in futility, a great fallacy, an unrealizable chimera, the answer must be that it is far more dangerous and impractical not to disarm. With thermonuclear bombs loose in a lawless world, with an arms race which has acquired an irresistible momentum of its own, disarmament becomes a necessity of world life. Disarmament becomes no longer a dream of the idealist but a matter of intense practical concern. Disarmament is not a pious, sentimental hope; it is the only remaining, practical, pragmatic approach to peace that is available to the peoples of the world today; it is the only key left in our ring to open the door to the road to peace, to create that framework of nonviolence within which nations can work out their clashes of interest. Disarmament is the prerequisite, the essential beginning of the long journey toward world peace.

In the quest for peace, no realistic course is left except that of disarmament. This course has no particular ideological content that would alienate East or West; in fact it is already the avowed goal of both the Soviet Union and the United States, as well as of the neutralist nations. Since the doctrine already boasts a large body of respectable scientific and public support, these public testaments bespeak a climate in world opinion to which one can appeal.

It is interesting to note that Sir Winston Churchill was led to the same solution to the dilemma of mankind. He told the House of Commons on March 1, 1955, "What ought we to do? Which way shall we turn to save our lives and the future of the world? It does not matter so much to old people. They are going soon anyway. But I find it poignant to look at youth in all its activities and ardor; and most of all, to watch little children playing their merry games, and wonder what would lie before them if God wearied of mankind. The best defense would, of course, be bona fide disarmament all around."

It has been said that "human history becomes more and more a race between education and catastrophe." Beyond doubt, as of today, catastrophe is far in the lead in this race. "The cannon speaks in the teacher's place."

The story is told that a reporter broke the news of the dropping of the Hiroshima bomb to Albert Einstein as the scientist was returning from sailing on Saranac Lake. The startled Einstein asked, "Do you mean that, young man?" Assured that it was so, Einstein slowly shook his head, and after a pause, made only one comment: "Ach! The world is not ready for it."

President Johnson echoed the same sentiments to the United Nations General Assembly on December 17, 1963: "Our understanding of how to live—live with one another —is still far behind our knowledge of how to destroy one another." Speaking to the House of Commons on November 22, 1945, soon after the dropping of the atomic bombs on Japan, Anthony Eden eloquently formulated the dilemma of this age: "The truth is that by the discovery of this atomic energy, science has placed us several laps ahead of every present phase of international political development, and unless we catch up politically to the point we have reached in science, and thus command the power which at present threatens us, we are all going to be blown to smithereens."

The truth also is that, in the interim between 1945 and the present, man has not matured politically to sufficiently close the gap opened by the advances of science. If anything, the pace of technological progress has made the gap much wider. Man is still woefully unprepared to exercise the lordship which he has assumed over the life and death of all living things. Where adulthood is necessary for peace, man is still struggling with the childlike mentality which is only appropriate for war.

Dr. Albert Schweitzer, in his speech of November 4, 1954, in which he accepted the Nobel Peace Prize, stated, "Man became superman with the aid of science. But the superman has not raised himself to the level of super-human reason. . . . The more we become supermen, the more we become inhuman." Not only has man failed to mature politically; he has also failed to develop emotion-ally and socially to the level of maturity required by the atomic age.

General Omar N. Bradley told the Boston Chamber of Commerce on November 10, 1948: "With the monstrous weapons man already has, humanity is in danger of being trapped in this world by its moral adolescents. . . . Man is stumbling blindly through a spiritual darkness while toying with the precarious secrets of life and death. The world has achieved brilliance without wisdom, power without conscience. Ours is a world of nuclear giants and ethical infants. We know more about war than about peace; more about killing than we know about living."

Technologically we are living in an atomic age while emotionally we are still living in the Stone Age. Man must have time to reach maturity. William Benton posed the question, "Is there time for the human race to avoid blast-ing itself and its seed into eternal, gibbering night?"

Realizing that the hydrogen bomb has wiped out time; the citizen must, nevertheless, insist on buying sufficient time to avoid catastrophe. That time can be bought only by disarmament. The entire purpose of disarmament is to gain time to permit mankind to mature as much politi-cally and emotionally as he has scientifically. Only dis-armament is capable of holding off a war until man's edu-cation draws even in the race with catastrophe. It should be clear that unless the arms race is first stopped, that race will be lost by forfeit. There is no other known method that will give the world the required time to work its way out of its present critical dilemma. Disarmament is certainly not the end-all in man's quest for peace; but it, undoubtedly, is a required way station.

Therefore, the citizen must echo President Eisenhower's farewell address in insisting that the conference table, "though scarred by many past frustrations, cannot be abandoned for the certain agony of the battlefield." Regardless of how discouraging arms-control negotiations may become, public opinion must never accept their discontinuance. It is a continuing imperative that the diplomats remain at the conference table because, while they are still talking, their countrymen will not be fighting.

In calling for disarmament, we mean honest, true, bona fide disarmament—not the specious kind of disarmament that has been discussed at international conferences. To describe that concept, even the word "disarmament" has been discarded, and a new semantic term has been coined —"arms control." As we have seen in our review of negotiations before and after World War II, the aims of arms control and the aims of national military strategy are substantially the same. Whether the idea is called "arms control" or "minarmament" or "arms stabilization at lower levels," it is clear that arms control is a theory of armaments; not of disarmament. As a matter of fact, the whole doctrine of arms control is a manual in how *not* to disarm.

The proponents of this theory see, in the strategic nuclear balance, a natural resting place of the arms race on which a system of international security through arms control might be built. Arms control is thus part and parcel of the whole theory of deterrence. It is its business to continue the nuclear stalemate by institutionalizing, preserving and buttressing the sanctity of the existing balance of power. It cannot be shaped by any such scatter-brain principle as the indiscriminate reduction of armaments. It is interesting to note that many of the same people who advocate arms control are working feverishly to break through the arms stalemate. The billions of dollars being spent on war research can only result in upsetting the existing stability of balance.

This is illustrated by the consternation which struck proponents of arms control when it was learned that the United States Joint Chiefs of Staff had unanimously recommended the production and deployment of an anti-missile missile defense system at a cost of $40 billion. A major research and development program, under way for seven years and involving the expenditure of more than $2 billion, had devised a highly effective anti-ballistic missile (ABM) Sentinel system involving astonishing new radars, computers and nuclear-tipped interceptor Spartan and Sprint missiles.

Spartan is designed to blast enemy warheads while they are still 50-400 miles up in space. Since a warhead will hit its target in less than 60 seconds from that height, Spartan has less than one minute to sort out the real warhead from the decoys and to get its prey. Work is progressing to equip Spartan with a Spectrum Warhead designed to give off X-rays so as to provide area defense. The inner ring hypersonic (supersonic is not good enough) Sprint would be a nation's final insurance policy. In order to stop enemy warheads at heights of 20-40 miles, Sprint is literally exploded from its silo launcher by a solid fuel piston, built into the launcher, at a speed of several thousand miles an hour. Even then, studies indicate that, in a massive attack, the leakage rate of warheads able to penetrate through the ABM screen would range between 60 and 70 per cent.

Work is also going forward in the United States on the development of an advanced surface-to-air missile (SAM-D) designed to fill both battlefield and continental air defense roles. Secretary Brezhnev had previously announced "important steps" in the anti-missile field and Soviet Galosh and Griffon ABM missiles had been paraded in Red Square.

Since by Pentagon calculations, in the absence of an ABM defense, a Soviet attack in 1970 would kill 149,000,-000 Americans, Secretary Clifford is confronted with a harrowing dilemma in deciding whether to postpone or go ahead with a full-scale anti-missile program. It is estimated that such a program would save 50 million lives and enable roughly one-half of the industrial capacity and retaliatory missile force to survive.

Because the ABM's would carry nuclear warheads, which would be exploded in a vast defensive cone of fire high above national territory to destroy oncoming enemy ICBM's, an extensive fallout shelter program would be an essential adjunct of this damage- limiting program. These shelters would cost another $5 billion. It is the opinion of experts that, without these shelters, 30 per cent more lives might be lost from radioactive debris.

Fearful that this program would have destabilized the existing precarious deterrent balance and trigger a new arms spiral, a high-level citizens' panel of the White House Conference on International Cooperation urged in 1966 a three-year delay. The Congress was again unwilling to wait. It nudged a hesitant Administration into faster development and deployment of the anti-missile system by appropriating unwanted hundreds of millions of dollars.

The die was cast when former Secretary McNamara divulged, at the LBJ Ranch in Texas on November 10, 1966, that intelligence advice indicated that the Russians were deploying a massive missile defense arc around Moscow and Leningrad and a second lighter interception Tallinn System covering the missile window across the northwestern part of the Soviet Union. President Johnson then attempted, without success, to get negotiations going with Soviet leaders regarding the possibility of mutual limitations on both offensive and defensive missiles. The Russians refused, claiming that their missiles were defensive.

Finally, Mr. McNamara, in an address to editors of United Press International in San Francisco on September 18, 1967, announced the Administration's decision. It was to go ahead—not with a heavy Russian-oriented anti-ballistic missile deployment, but with a $5 billion thin missile net designed to protect American cities against light missile attacks of the type the Chinese will be able to launch in the mid-1970's. The *New York Times* commented editorially that the proposed system was probably designed for defense against the Republicans as much as against the Chinese Communists.

The illusory balance of nuclear security is thus teetering at another threshold. Another destablizing factor portends a new upward spiral, a quantum jump. Once again, a small commitment blossoms into a program that develops a life of its own. Each year it expands, leading to new counter-programs by the Soviets which lead to still other counter-programs by the Americans which lead to . . .

The most frightening aspect of the Soviet-American

military equation is the inexorable rhythm of its measures and countermeasures. For, admittedly, it may not appear so clear to the Russians that the ABM system is in fact being built primarily to cope with Red China. Indeed, Defense Secretary Clark M. Clifford has so indicated. Apparently, then, the old "action-reaction phenomenon" will fuel a newly accelerated arms race. The tragedy is that it is conceded that "none of the systems at the present or foreseeable state of the art would provide an impenetrable shield over the United States" and that the decision was taken on "marginal grounds."

Scientific critics maintain that any antiballistic missile system that can now be produced represents a kind of Maginot Line—an imagined security. No ABM system can be leakproof. No matter what the Russian response, it is certain that the weapons cultists will press to expand the projected thin ABM system into a heavy Soviet-oriented net. This will occur despite the warning of Mr. McNamara that "I know of nothing we could do today that would waste more of our resources or add more to our risks."

One paragraph of the ex-Secretary's San Francisco speech should be quoted and re-quoted: "It is futile for each of us to spend $4 billion, $40 billion, or $400 billion —and at the end of all the spending, and at the end of all the deployment, and at the end of all the effort, to be relatively at the same point of balance on the security scale that we are now."

There have been earlier plateaus and earlier disruptions of the neat equations of balance in the rising crescendo of destructive capabilities which marks the nuclear age. First, we had the primitive, rudimentary atom bomb of

Hiroshima and Nagasaki. Then, as the Russians caught up with the technique of producing these hellish weapons, there was a period of moderate stability. This was followed by the climb to the height of the more sophisticated thermonuclear bomb and a new period of high instability. The Russians again balanced the scales with their own H bomb. From that balance, mankind advanced to the present point of no return of the solid fuel, hardened ICBM. To what new pinnacle will the threatened vertical proliferation of ABM weapon systems and the countering MIRV's lead us?

In many ways, then, arms control is a fatalistic doctrine. It is a counsel of despair in holding out no hope that mankind can ever escape from under the sword of Damocles. At best, the doctrine is a symbolic euphemism, a refusal to come to grips with and to grapple with the greatest challenge of our age. At worst, the doctrine is a fraud and a deceit, a sop to the countless millions who are staking their lives on the outcome of the disarmament negotiations.

When the United States delegate to the seventeen-nation conference declares that the bonfire of obsolete bombers would give a "graphic example of armament reduction to the entire world," he insults that world's intelligence. Unfortunately, most of the other arms control measures that have been proposed are equally meaningless and dishonestly motivated.

Since this book is concerned with a disarmament agreement which, by definition, requires bilateral negotiation, we unfortunately will not be discussing unilateral disarmament. This does not mean that there isn't much to be said for unilateral action of a tension-reducing nature.

It may well be that the great moral force of unilateral disarmament is the only practical way of achieving an unarmed world.

The sad fact is that there is no half-way house to disarmament; no piecemeal measures that can avail to remove so monstrous an evil as the threat of war. Here is one instance where half a loaf is not better than none. For this is one of those rare and tragic moments of history where there is no acceptable middle way. Thus, a lower level of armaments does not necessarily mean a lower level of danger.

Mr. McNamara has admitted that both the United States and the Soviet Union have more warheads than they had originally planned, and that they in fact require. Suppose the West has 80,000 nuclear bombs and the East 30,000. Would it be a source of real comfort if these stockpiles were reduced to 40,000 and 15,000, if each of the remaining bombs could raze a city and destroy a million people? In either case, the possible scale of suffering and damage is absolutely beyond human comprehension.

The terrible thing is that each side's program of stockpiling massive weapons passed the point of diminishing returns long ago. Indeed, as far as partial disarmament is concerned, it was not only the point of diminishing returns, but the point of no return which was passed. All those additional absolute, overkill weapons, held by each grotesquely overarmed side, are so absolutely useless that armaments have crossed the boundary from rationality to absurdity. Any partial disarmament that would conceivably be agreed to by either side would still leave each side with more than enough firepower to overkill every living thing many times over. For each side to reduce to enough armaments to kill each other only once would require too drastic a cut.

In negotiating any program of partial or gradual disarmament, the diplomats run head-on into myriads of insoluble equations. For instance, what exchange value is assignable to a tank as compared to a foot soldier, or a supersonic fighter plane, or a PT boat, or a Polaris missile? The ancient Indians once estimated one chariot as equal to one elephant, three cavalrymen or five infantry men. What Descartes could devise a magical, universally acceptable index that would equate the relative values of these military ingredients? One begins to realize how it is almost impossible to negotiate a scale of comparison for different weapon systems.

Even if the diplomats could, by some miracle, agree on a ratio of military values, since all the hardware cannot be destroyed at the same time, how could the signatories ever agree on a timetable of weapon destruction? The questions of stages and phasing could wreck any substantive agreement. So long as one talks about anything less than total disarmament, each step must be taken with an eye to war; because if the agreement breaks down, each side must be ready to fight. Each government must thus propose first steps which are unfair to its opponents or be guilty of treason. We have seen, in practice, the actual operation of this theory.

Nor does a disarmament treaty seem possible so long as the doctrine of arms control pervades the thinking of the diplomats. Since the purpose of treaties of arms control is not to abolish military power, but to stabilize a military situation, one is confronted with the insoluble problem. What is the military situation at any given moment? How could the imprecise and constantly changing military balance, which exists in the real world and in the calculations and anxieties of statesmen, ever be translated into the precision and fixity of a treaty? Does this dynamic military technology lend itself to regulation along traditional diplomatic lines?

Further, a solution along hardware lines seems doomed to failure because of the continuous emergence of new devices. No partial reduction of forces, however scrupulously carried out, could protect the powers against a technological breakthrough. Science cannot be frozen.

Nor can we term disarmament proposals the many bizarre schemes that have been suggested by many well-meaning men, with the most honest of intentions, in desperation, as means of breaking through the vicious circle of failure of negotiations. One plan would divide each country into roughly equivalent checkerboard squares with reciprocal squares to be cleared of arms simultaneously. Another idea, that of "mined cities," was set forth in the December 1961 issue of the *Bulletin of the Atomic Scientists* by the late Dr. Leo Szilard, then of the University of Chicago. Nuclear demolition teams would be planted in caverns beneath opposing Soviet and American cities. This would work as a safety valve and each nation could then let off steam by exchanging pawns, like blowing up Minneapolis in a swap for Minsk, or Denver for Dnepropetrovsk.

In a proposal reminiscent of the ancients, Stephen D. James introduced a peace hostage exchange program. Prominent American and Soviet citizens would be exchanged as hostage guarantees against the possibility of nuclear attack. The children of the national leaders could be traded as the most precious hostages. Thomas Schelling even proposed that American and Soviet kindergarten classes be exchanged each year.

The whole concept of hostages is a very tempting idea. Why not turn the tables? Instead of millions of people being hostages for their governments and their leaders, why not make the leaders stand hostage instead? A corps of trained, neutral assassins could be provided with an observer stationed at the side of each leader with the power to make war. If the statesman steps out of line, the assassin has the authority to shoot him. How much less costly in lives such a scheme would be.

Or perhaps the nations might deliberately exchange spies to facilitate the transmission of authentic information. It has even been proposed that national leaders be permanently wired to lie detectors and other electronic devices so that cheating or aggressive intentions might be instantly detected.

We have already seen how it is possible to advance such crazy schemes, or arms control, or partial disarmament, or disarmament by stages—none of which has anything to do with disarmament—in the holy name of disarmament. We have discussed the military motivation behind disarmament negotiations and how these international quadrilles permit the vested military-industrial complexes to eat their cakes and have them, too.

But these schemes and proposals serve another very important purpose. They create an illusion of activity for that part of the public opinion which is impatiently looking over the shoulders of the diplomats. But the public has not been let in on the rules of the game and is ignorant of the facts of life. And since each scheme is a reflection of the suspicion, distrust, hate and fear in which the adversary is held, the excuse for failure comes built into the proposal. Because each side knows, within its heart, that it will begin to connive and cheat before the ink on any agreement is dry, each attributes similar intentions to the other side.

This pervading atmosphere of suspicion, which blankets every disarmament conference, dooms in advance any scheme of partial or graded disarmament. Any disarmament agreement, like any commercial contract, must be grounded on trust and confidence in the honorable intentions of both parties.

The interminable conferences have demonstrated the insurmountable difficulties confronting partial or piecemeal solutions to the disarmament problem. Thus, it should be infinitely easier to arrive at agreement on complete disarmament than on partial measures. There is no other method of tearing negotiations free from the detail that gives rise to bickering and legal pettifogging. Ultimately, there is only one bona fide practicable outcome that can break the logjam of the stalemated disarmament negotiations. There is only one way to cut the Gordian knot and take the weapons from the hands of the psychopaths. There is only one answer. That answer, strangely enough, is that disarmament means disarmament—general and complete, total and universal. Armaments must be reduced to the police level with a complete scrapping of nuclear weapons—down to what Sir Winston Churchill termed "pikes and maces."

This answer should not sound too startling or revolutionary. It is the declared and avowed policy of both the United States and the Soviet Union. In a joint statement of principles made to the United Nations by these two powers on September 20, 1961, they declared, "The goal of negotiation is to ensure that disarmament is general and complete and war is no longer an instrument for settling international problems . . . that states will have at their disposal only those non-nuclear armaments as are agreed to be necessary to maintain internal order."

Every human endeavor involves a certain degree of risk. Short of universal brain surgery, nothing can erase the memory of weapons and how to build them. Thus, any agreement for meaningful disarmament requires, ultimately, an act of faith.

It should be evident, by now, that only the romanticists still believe that modern armaments can make a nation safe. In the words of President Kennedy, "The risks inherent in disarmament pale in comparison to the risks inherent in an unlimited arms race." No matter how great a risk we run in advocating general and complete disarmament, the alternative, an uncontrolled situation and a collision course toward war, involves far greater risks—risks that are total and eternal. The risks of doing nothing are also fearful.

One must deplore, with Dr. Jerome B. Wiesner, dean of science at the Massachusetts Institute of Technology, the tendency "to judge arms control in the light of the most dangerous possibility, no matter how unlikely, and to give no weight at all to the consequences of failing to halt the arms race."

Bona fide disarmament offers far more security and far fewer risks than an unabated, unpredictable arms race, because while we pursue that race, we are literally playing with the eternal fire. The only real security is the security that will come with total disarmament, safe-guarded by inspection and control. The security of each nation will date from the moment when the United Nations inspector takes up his post; in the same manner that the security of the urban citizen began when the policeman started to walk his beat.

11

Disarmament by the People

Given the will, it is so laughably simple to accomplish total disarmament in one fell swoop that the whole thing is almost ludicrous. Disarmament is not an impossible dream. We can have disarmament now, today, tomorrow, next week, next month—any time that the people wish it.

Arms are instruments of evil. They are designed to kill. As such, they violate every moral code ever formulated by civilized man. "Thou shalt not kill," proclaims the Sixth Commandment. The evil was great when weapons could kill one man at a time. How much greater, then, is the crime today when modern scientific weapons permit the shattering of entire cities.

Aggregations of arms are useful for only one purpose —to fight wars. The mere accumulation of arms is an act of war. The smooth-talking salesmen and pleaders for the various Armed Services have sold the citizen a bill of goods that these lethal weapons are really doves of peace. Examine the merchandise and you must see that we have been cheated and hoodwinked. Even worse, we have been corrupted. To quote Loys Masson, "Satan has become tangible. He was made flesh at Hiroshima and every day strengthens and fattens him."

The highest religious authorities have anathematized the arms race and the massing of arms. For instance, the Ecumenical Council Vatican II declared in its Pastoral Constitution on the "Church in the Modern World:" "Whatever be the facts about this method of deterrence, men should be convinced that the arms race in which an already considerable number of countries are engaged is not a safe way to preserve a steady peace, nor is the so-called balance resulting from this race a sure and authentic peace. Rather than being eliminated thereby, the causes of war are in danger of being gradually aggravated."

The schema goes on to say, "The arms race is an utterly treacherous trap for humanity . . . It is much to be feared that if this race persists, it will eventually spawn all the lethal ruin whose path it is now making ready."

The same document sets forth the attitude of the Catholic Church towards war and acts of war in these words: "All these considerations compel us to undertake an evaluation of war with an entirely new attitude. The men of our time must realize that they will have to give a somber reckoning of their deeds of war, for the course of the future will depend greatly on the decisions they make today.

"With these truths in mind, this most holy synod makes its own the condemnations of total war already pronounced by recent Popes, and issues the following declaration:

"Any act of war aimed indiscriminately at the destruction of entire cities or of extensive areas along with their population is a crime against God and man himself. It merits unequivocal and unhesitating condemnation."

The National Council of Churches addressed the following "Message to Churches" on December 3, 1965: "As Christian members of a world-wide Christian family we must remind ourselves and our Government of these convictions: 1. We believe that war in this nuclear age settles hardly anything and may destroy everything."

The consensus of the civilized world has condemned war and the preparation for war. Then why is mankind continuing, without abatement, to manufacture more and more arms, to stockpile more and more terrible arms, to enslave more and more of our men through conscription to use these arms, to search for ever more fiendish arms? The fault, dear Brutus, lies with ourselves— the people— and with the leaders whom we have set upon or permitted to sit on the leopardskin throne.

It is probably too late to expect our leaders to head off the mad dash toward mutual annihilation. They have fed at the flesh-pots for too long. The politico-military-industrial complex is too wedded to the system of war—too much a part and parcel of the whole arms race—to change the direction of current history. It is our leaders who are building and stockpiling these immoral arms. It is our leaders who are threatening to unleash the foul force of atomic arms upon our heads. It is our leaders who are perpetrating these grievous crimes against God and man. Certainly, we cannot expect these same criminals to turn from their ways of sin towards the path of righteousness. Certainly, we can't expect them to give the command to ground arms.

It, therefore, remains for those who are threatened by the wanton actions of these criminals to act in self defense. Those who are threatened are, of course, you and me, the citizens, the people.

Perhaps even that possibility is too late. Perhaps we have become habituated to horror. Perhaps we have been so brutalized by the stench of so much killing for so many centuries that our moral sense has been dulled forever.

Imagine, however, if the people, for once, stopped marching in tandem, like sheep, and rose up, in all their majesty, in outraged wrath and indignation to command the criminals: "ENOUGH! HALT, STOP, CEASE, DESIST, from this madness forthwith!"

Imagine if the people were to pause, for just a few moments, to reflect upon where they are going and what the probable outcome is. In the course of this reflection, the people must ask themselves how else their country might be defended, aside from through the force of arms.

What is the alternative? The answer must be that whatever policy is right, the use of arms is wrong. The arms race demands no more detailed alternative for the people to reject it than did Stalin's blood baths or Hitler's gas chambers. An arms policy comes from the same corner of Hell. It is unworthy of sane human beings.

Philip Noel-Baker has declared that disarmament can be achieved in one week if the people can only be mobilized. Once the peoples of the world realize that atomic incineration need not be their inevitable fate, no nation will be able to withstand the force of public opinion demanding disarmament forthwith. "All I ask," with Albert Camus, "is that, in the midst of a murderous world, we agree to reflect on murder and make a choice."

As one of the people, the individual soldier should also

pause and reflect upon what he is doing. Why is he holding that weapon in his hand? Is it to kill his brother or
his brother's bride or his brother's child or his brother's
sister or his brother's parent? If the individual soldier
reflects upon it, he will realize that he is committing a
mortal sin. The weapon he holds in his hand is unclean.
He, together with the rest of the people, should demand
that that weapon be dropped forthwith. In the words of
the Holy Father, Pope Paul VI, "If you wish to be brothers, let the arms fall from your hands. One cannot love
while holding offensive arms."

As one of the people, the soldier, stationed at a fort
or a military installation, should also pause and reflect
upon what he is doing. Why have these huge stockpiles
of munitions been massed in this place? Is it to rain fire,
death and destruction upon his fellow men? The place
he inhabits is an unholy place, a pesthole spreading pestilence and disease to the population. He, together with
the rest of the people, should demand that the installation
be quarantined, avoided like the plague, abandoned forthwith to the rats.

As one of the people, the soldier, billeted away from
home on foreign soil, should also pause and reflect upon
what he is doing. Why is he living in this unnatural way,
away from his home and his loved ones, in a land where
he is unwelcome? His place and duty are at home, where
his mother, his wife and his children await him with
loving arms. Why should he postpone living? He, together
with the rest of the people, should demand that he be
returned forthwith to where he belongs, to where he can
live a productive life.

As one of the people, the cadet, enrolled in a military
academy, should also pause and reflect upon what he is

doing. What is he studying here? Is it to be a savage, to kill innocent men, women and children? Certainly, there is no more monstrous study and no more nefarious vocation to which one can dedicate one's life. He, together with the rest of the people, should demand that these classes be disbanded forthwith.

As one of the people, the scientist, toiling in his laboratory, should also pause and reflect upon what he is doing. Is he concocting new and more fiendish ways to torture and murder living souls and eventually obliterate life itself? Is that the purpose for which he devoted years of monastic poring over books and test tubes? If he has a conscience, why isn't he following the example of the Russian atomic scientist Kapitza who suffered years under house arrest because he refused to work on atomic bombs? The scientist, together with the rest of the people, should demand that his talents be diverted from the pursuit of death to the pursuit of life.

As one of the people, the worker, the manager, the investor in munition works should also pause and reflect upon what he is doing. What is he manufacturing in that plant? Are they devices for laying bare the skulls and flesh of persons like himself, whom he does not know, whom he has never seen, with whom he has no quarrel? Perchance, this same hellish projectile may find its target in his own loved one. Certainly, a man has lost all sense of humanity when he offers to produce such instruments of the devil for a mess of blood-stained money. He, together with the rest of the people, should demand that the resources of industry be converted forthwith to supply the needs of the billions on this earth who are in dire need.

The citizen, as a citizen of the world, should pause and

reflect how the incredible beauty and wonder of this planet have been converted into today's obscene horror of a nuclear powder keg. Who have been the architects of this blasphemous alchemy? Could it be that our leaders —those reasonable, decent bureaucrats who are the very incarnation of rationality—have, in their single-minded specialization, lost contact with us? Could it be that, in their single-minded devotion to their nation, they have unknowing crossed the line into insanity? Why, else, has the world become a madhouse?

The modern world resembles nothing so much as an old frontier wild West town. Desperadoes gallop up and down the dusty streets, shooting everything up at will. Either the decent citizens abandon the town or they come to the end of their patience and impose a rule of law and order.

Having lost patience with the killing and the endless negotiations, the peoples should demand that the representatives of the nations of the world assemble forthwith in the United Nations to outlaw the instruments of war. The people should brush aside any piecemeal or token solution. They must not compromise, they must not equivocate. They must insist that the only way to disarm is to disarm. They will not be satisfed with anything less than general, complete, universal and total disarmament, enforced by full inspection and control.

The resolution of the United Nations should summarily outlaw all arms (outside of small police arms necessary to maintain internal order), their possession, their production, their research as of an early date, preferably the first of the subsequent year.

To stress the overriding importance of the United Nations resolution and to dramatize its adoption, its terms should provide for ratification by referendum of the peoples of the world on a one man, one vote basis. The disarmament would become effective when approved by two-thirds of the persons voting. In the same way that no individual can unilaterally remove himself from the authority of the police in any jurisdiction, once the treaty is ratified, no nation will have the power to withdraw from its coverage.

This provision differs from the Test Ban Treaty. Article IV of that treaty provides that a party may withdraw on three months notice where "extraordinary events, related to the subject matter of this treaty, have jeopardized the supreme interests of its country." In our proposed treaty, no nation will be able to opt out from this world.

The disarmament convention would operate in a manner similar to the one of 1965 outlawing racial discrimination, with built-in enforcement procedures to be legally binding on the subject states. Thus, prior to the effective date, each nation shall be required to adopt reciprocal legislation outlawing armaments. Further, before that date, each nation would be obliged to demobilize its armed forces completely and return the men to their homes. Police contingents would have to be reduced to a fixed percentage of the population—say .25 per cent. General staffs would have to be disbanded and all military schools closed. All weapons, delivery mechanisms, nuclear devices, military vehicles and other military paraphernalia are either to be adapted to civilian use or stacked and abandoned. All forts, missile sites and military installations are to be abandoned. All national budgets would have to be revised to eliminate completely any defense appropriations.

In the interim, prior to the effective date, the United

Nations would be recruiting an international police and inspection force. The world agency would also be adding a judicial arm to its organizational torso with all the attendant appurtenances of a supreme court, regional courts, prosecutors, prisons, police and so on. The personnel would be professional international civil servants, with tenure, owing allegiance only to the United Nations. A limit would be imposed on the percentage of nationals from any one country.

On that great and glorious day, which will thenceforth be celebrated as Peace Day instead of New Year's Day, each country will hand over to the United Nations inspection force a complete inventory of the military establishment still located on its territory, together with all blueprints and other data pertaining thereto. It shall then become the responsibility of the international force to dispose of the weaponry.

Beginning with the Peace Day, it shall be declared a heinous crime for any—repeat, any—individual, to possess, manufacture, perform research upon, transport, install, store, test, acquire, or handle any weapon other than sidearms of a police type. The term "weapon" would be broadly defined to include delivery vehicles and systems along with chemical, biological, radiological and other death-dealing devices. The aim is disengagement, the complete separation of man from his weapons. In the words of Lao-Tse, "weapons are not instruments of joy, but objects of hatred to every creature. Therefore, he who has Tao will not stay where they are."

By the terms of the mutual treaties, the United Nations and the various states will pledge themselves to launch a vast educational campaign to impress upon the people that the international disarmament agreement is mankind's shield against mutual extermination. Therefore, violation will be a capital crime against humanity because it endangers the lives of everyone. War toys will no longer be permitted. From that blessed day henceforth, the world will no longer know war between nations. War will be a curiosity read about in history books and viewed in horror museums, such as the one in Hiroshima.

In pressing for the kind of treaty that we are describing here, the people are not pretending that they are thereby abolishing all rivalry and conflict between nations. The people just want to try to make sure that this rivalry and conflict will not abolish them. The intent is to make war impossible by removing its means. The nations will just have to devise other methods than war for resolving their disputes—perhaps arbitration. Imagine how more productive international conferences would be if the present jungle atmosphere of tenseness, suspicion and imminent catastrophe were dissipated. Imagine if the diplomat did not have to keep in mind the fact that the other side was simultaneously working feverishly on ever more fearful means of destruction and surprise attack.

The treaty is primarily directed towards preventing wars between nations. United Nations inspectors would have no authority in civil wars beyond ascertaining that the arms limitations are respected. However, it is hoped that the habit of peaceful settlement will eventually spread to internecine disputes.

Obviously, the disarmament treaty can be sketched here only in the broadest details. The entire idea is to set a standard. As Aneurin Beven said, there is no greater mistake in politics than to try to foresee and provide in advance for every contingency.

The idea of a treaty to outlaw war is not original. There

have been many such compacts, of which the Kellogg Pact of 1928 is a good example. That treaty taught us a lesson, however, and the lesson is that no agreement is worth the paper upon which it is written unless it provides for sanctions. Sanctions may, for our purposes, be defined as punishment in case of violation. These sanctions are the key to the effectiveness of any treaty.

Here we have proposed a treaty of general and complete disarmament. How shall it be enforced? Amitai Etzioni poses a hypothetical instance. Suppose the treaty has gone into force and the international inspection service has gone into operation. A neutral inspector accidentally opens a door in a hangar next to a Russian airport in the far Urals and stumbles over 100 hidden nuclear bombs. What then?

Shall enforcement be *in rem?* That is, shall the remedy of the United Nations be restricted to confiscation of the bombs?

Or, shall charges be filed against Russia with the new United Nations judiciary? Suppose, after a fair trial, Russia is found guilty and fined an enormous sum. Suppose Russia then refuses to pay. Or better still, suppose Russia refuses to even submit to trial. We have put our finger on the precise flaw which has caused so many other treaties to fail. In the last analysis, the only way to enforce sanctions against a government is to go to war, which is just what we are trying to avoid in the first place.

Nor is it just to proceed against an entire country or a whole people. Such a method punishes the innocent along with the guilty. We have seen that no whole people is evil or war-mongering or criminal. The overwhelming majority of the people in any country are toilers of muscle and brain who only ask that they be left alone to make a living for themselves and their families. The purpose of any law enforcement is to distinguish between those individuals who are guilty and those who are not.

Besides, that is the whole purpose of this treaty—to separate the few, ambitious, warring leaders from the great peace-loving mass of humanity. The treaty codifies the principle that humanity is above all nations. To that end, since the nations have abused their sovereignty and brought the earth to the very brink of obliteration, the people are demanding that each nation surrender a portion of its sovereignty.

In order to prevent war and preparation for war, the United Nations must be vested with sufficient attributes of sovereignty to accomplish this single purpose. In this respect, then, the United Nations will take on the authority of a government instead of a league. As a government, the authority of the United Nations will extend to the persons of the citizens of the world—the only proper objects of government.

Thus, in our hypothetical situation, the United Nations police will proceed to investigate how the bombs found their way to their cache and who the individuals are who are responsible for the horde. Of course, the bombs would be confiscated. But, in addition, the guilty persons—no matter how high their station in the Russian government —would be brought to justice.

Thus, the prohibition in our treaty would run not against the hardware or the government, but against the individual. Our treaty will impose upon every individual of the world a responsibility, concurrent and simultaneous with that of his government, to rid himself of any prohibited weapon. Like the Sullivan Act in New York State, the possession of such a weapon *ipso facto* constitutes a crime. Nor will the international tribunal accept as a justification for that possession an Adolf Eichmann type plea that the accused was acting under orders. For so atrocious a crime as threatening the lives of one's brothers there is no excuse before either God or man.

Further, the treaty would impose an obligation upon each individual to report immediately any violation. The methods of inspection will be discussed more fully in later chapters.

It is realized that many objects—such as dynamite, jet planes, jeeps, trucks, etc.—may be used for both warlike and peaceful purposes. The crime is committed the instant a peaceful facility is converted to military use. The test, as in all crime, is one of motive—a factor which would have to be proven by the prosecution.

In the same way that narcotics traffic, kidnapping and prostitution are both state and federal offenses in the United States, the crime outlined here would be a violation of both national and international law and punishable by either or both. The Nuremberg trials set the precedent for international authority.

Only then will mankind achieve the objectives outlined by Justice Robert H. Jackson in his opening address to the International Military Tribunal established to try the war crimes: "The ultimate step in avoiding periodic wars, which are inevitable in a system of international lawlessness, is to make statesmen responsible to law . . . . This trial represents mankind's desperate effort to apply the discipline of the law to statesmen who have used their powers of state to attack the foundations of the world's peace and to commit aggression against the rights of their neighbors." Under our proposed treaty, the individual will come to the fore as the proper object of restraint and punishment for international crimes.

James Bryce once said, "Feeling the law to be its own work, the people are disposed to obey the law." The negotiation of the disarmament treaties and the passage of the concurrent national legislation would, in themselves, go a long way towards winning the nations to the rule of peace. The mere fact that disarmament takes on an aura of legality is important. That is the mystic foundation of the authority of law. Few men are willing to place themselves outside the pale of the law because man is basically law-abiding. In the words of Chairman Khrushchev, "If some side violates the agreement it assumed, the instigators of this violation will cover themselves with shame, they will be condemned by the peoples of the whole world."

The proposed disarmament treaty could very well be the beginning of civilized manners among nations.

It is the purpose of our disarmament treaty to reduce human suffering: not to create new hardships. Transition measures will be required to cushion the transition of demobilized soldiers and discharged workers from war to peace activities. Those who are capable of work should be retrained at government expense with no loss of pay. The $130 billion allotted annually for war preparations should provide a more than ample fund to smooth whatever temporary dislocations have been suffered by these persons.

Fortunately, the underdeveloped countries of the world

provide a frontier which will require the dedicated efforts of all these persons, and more, for decades to come. Literally billions of our fellow men lack the absolute basic necessities of food, clothing, shelter, health and education.

Imagine if the engineering corps turned to construction of homes and roads and schools and hospitals and dams and bridges. Imagine if the naval vessels could be converted to power plants for the immense areas which lack electricity. Imagine if the jeeps and trucks were diverted to carry food and other necessities to market and to the countless villages on the globe. Imagine if the $130 billion wasted annually were devoted to bringing life and health and food and clothing and shelter to the underprivileged of the world. Imagine if, instead of producing missiles and bombs for ultimate delivery, we delivered butter, milk, meat, bread, soup and books. The deserts will bloom when the swords are finally beat into plowshares and the spears into pruning hooks.

The proposed treaty is obviously a gamble. All life is a gamble. But these gambles pale to nothingness compared to the greatest risk of all, which is war. If the people do not succeed in this attempt at disarmament, what have they lost over what they would have lost by inaction? The world cannot be left where it is. If the people do not try to destroy war, war will destroy them. Certainly, disarmament has been demonstrated to involve less risk to civilization and humanity than a continuation of the arms race.

Listen to the words of President Kennedy, as delivered at the commencement of American University in Washington on June 10, 1963: "No treaty, however much it may be to the advantage of all, however tightly it may be worded, can provide absolute security against the risks of deception and evasion. But it can—if it is sufficiently effective in its enforcement and it is sufficiently in the interests of its signers—offer far more security and far fewer risks than an unabated, uncontrolled, unpredictable arms race."

Specifically, what risks will be faced by the United States under the terms of our proposed treaty? Only two countries will pose any credible threat to the safety and security of the United States within the foreseeable future. Those two countries are the Soviet Union and Red China. It should be remembered first that the kind of treaty we are discussing could not even be possible unless the people in each of these countries had succeeded in changing the climate to one of accommodation.

The treaty would have to provide for open access and inspection from the date of signing. Disarmament would be carried out in full sight of both nations. Thus, the United States would be observing the Russian steps in compliance and would, undoubtedly, be pacing its measures accordingly. The possibility always exists that an over-zealous group of the military or some die-hard communists, who may doubt the ability of their way of life to conquer in peaceful competition, might conceal some atomic bombs. After all, we need only worry about the accountability of atomic weapons because conventional weapons could do only little harm.

What could these die-hards do with their atomic bombs? How could they deliver them 6,000 miles to the United States? What delivery system would they use? Jet planes, missiles and submarines are too bulky to be easily concealed, especially since in our system of inspection by the people, as explained later, all eyes will be alert for treaty breakers.

These die-hards would then be reduced to smuggling

the atomic devices into the United States in valises. This is possible because a strategic nuclear warhead can now be contained in a cylinder 5 feet long and 23½ inches in diameter. If one such terrorist succeeded in caching a bomb in Washington and then called on the government to surrender or else, the United States would be faced with a serious problem. That risk will just have to be weighed against the risk of total war.

Red China offers a different problem. Despite its centuries of ancient culture, politically this country is like an infant tearing off its swaddling clothes and thrashing about in its newly discovered strength. Naturally, Red China resents its containment by both the United States and the Soviet Union.

However, no settlement of the arms race and no disarmament agreement is possible without the concurrence of that Asiatic giant. To quote Secretary-General U Thant, "Progress in disarmament, whether general or nuclear, can hardly be made while one of the major military powers of the world which has recently become a nuclear power does not participate in the deliberations on such a serious subject." The United States will have to reappraise its Far Eastern policy and resign itself to the fact of international life that it occupies the same globe with China. The presence of one-fourth of the human race in the United Nations is required if that organization is ever to deal effectively with the problems of disarmament and peace. The United Nations, with all its faults, is the only existing world-peace-keeping agency and the one place where the disputes of the world can be resolved.

For all of its bluster, Red China is highly vulnerable to attack with massive dirty weapons. It has been calculated that half a billion Chinese could be destroyed in one night of nuclear terror. Further, she is still a desperately poor nation, with an annual per capita income of less than $100 per year. That country will achieve the basic necessities of life for its people so much sooner if she receives the cooperation, instead of the enmity, of the rest of the world. If the richer nations agreed to permit China to develop her own ideology, in her own way, without interference, and agreed to assist China financially and technically to advance economically, the probability is that the dragon would prove to be a paper one. Some readers will complain that this smacks of bribery. It is cheaper to give dollars than lives. A China that has advanced to the stage of goulash communism will not belch fire so recklessly.

What risks will be faced by the Soviet Union? If it is assumed that the American people do not want war, that assumption will certainly hold for the Russian people who are more familiar with the horrors of war. The Russians, too, will be monitoring the steps being taken by the Americans to comply with the disarmament treaty and they, too, will be responding in kind. They, too, face the risk that an over-zealous group of American military or some die-hard Birchites, who may doubt the ability of their free enterprise way of life to conquer in peaceful competition, might conceal some atomic bombs.

Suppose the Americans go through the motions of dropping their arms, abandoning their bases and disbanding their troops. The Russians, have, of course, done the same. Then suppose, after January 1, the Americans, acting on a secretly concocted plot, suddenly reassemble, seize the planes and missile sites which have not yet been destroyed by the United Nations and loose atomic ruin on the heads of the defenseless Russians.

This is a risk. There is no doubt that the world will have to sweat out an edgy period between the time the treaty is signed and the time the United Nations police force establishes control. The only answer would seem to be that the Soviet Union would have to absolutely saturate the United States and its overseas bases with observers. At the slightest suspicion of a violation, the Russians would also be free to resume its arms position. At that moment, the Secretary-General of the United Nations would have to step in to attempt to restore the operations of the treaty.

Of course, whatever is said above for the Russians would also hold true for the United States.

What risks will be faced by Red China? That country is now hopelessly outgunned in the race for atomic weapons. With general and complete disarmament, its horde of manpower would give it security, although it might menace its neighbors. That will be a particular risk affecting the Soviet Union, India and Pakistan that will have to be worked out somehow.

What risks will be faced by Western Europe? In the Cold War, they are sitting ducks for the first atomic bombardment of World War III. All they risk is their national grandeur.

And what of the great mass of other countries; what risks do they face? In the case of total atomic warfare, poisonous fallout will not respect any national boundaries. An African proverb states, "when the elephants fight, the grass is trampled." Under general and complete disarmament, the great resources of the richer countries will be invested in the underdeveloped lands. Only good can flow from such a turn of events.

The great sacrifice, in the event of general and complete disarmament, will be made by the revanchist generals, the atom rattling demagogues, the munition peddlers, the jingoists, the hate mongers, the war profiteers. Let us all shed a great big tear over their plight.

Better still, let us hearken to the great shout of the peoples, echoing and reechoing across the mountain tops of the earth, trumpeting forth the last command: "GROUND ARMS!"

12

The Story of Inspection

It is the popular impression that the Soviet Union has categorically rejected inspection as an integral part of any arms control agreement as "legalized espionage." The more kindly critics of Soviet policy explain that because of the profound imbalance of nuclear power in favor of the United States, the U.S.S.R. strenuously resists all efforts at reconnaissance and maintains geographical secrecy in order to protect its limited force.

In fact, however, the Soviet Union is on record only as opposing "controls without disarmament." It has been unwilling to exchange a large amount of inspection in return for a small amount of arms reduction. The U.S.S.R. has accepted, and indeed, proposed, inspection on innumerable occasions.

At the 1932 disarmament conference, Maxim Litvinov coupled his plan for general and complete disarmament with a statement that "very vigorous supervision should be established." On April 8, 1952, the Soviets agreed to an international control organization and simultaneous continuous inspection along with arms prohibition.

We have already discussed "the moment of hope" on May 10, 1955, when Jacob Malik accepted the Western plan and agreed to inspectors who "within the limits of the control function they exercise would have unhindered access at any time to all objects of control."

After the 1955 summit meeting, Marshal Bulganin told the Supreme Soviet, on August 4, 1955, that, "The President of the United States justly remarked that each disarmament plan boils down to the question of control and inspection."

In response to President Eisenhower's open skies proposal, the Soviet Union offered to open one-half of Siberia, together with non-Russian Europe, to inspection.

Chairman Khrushchev, in an address to the United Nations General Assembly, on September 19, 1959, declared, "If disarmament is comprehensive and complete, then, upon its attainment, control shall likewise be general and complete. No restraints will be imposed on the controllers' zeal because the states will have nothing to conceal from one another any more."

He was echoing the Declaration of the Soviet Government on Complete and General Disarmament: "The extent of the control and inspection exercised shall correspond to the stage reached in the phased disarmament of the States. Upon the completion of general and complete disarmament which shall include the disbandment of all types of weapons, including weapons of mass destruction (nuclear, rocket, chemical, bacteriological), the International Control Organ shall have free access to all objects of control."

The Camp David communiqué of President Eisenhower and Chairman Khrushchev stated that "each stage of disarmament should be accompanied by the development of inspection and control." Mr. Khrushchev pleaded in October 1960, "Agree to disarmament and we will agree to whatever controls you want."

The Joint Statement of Agreed Principles for Disarmament Negotiations submitted to the sixteenth General Assembly of the United Nations, on September 20, 1961, by the United States and the Soviet Union declared in Clause 6, as we have noted above: "All disarmament measures should be implemented from beginning to end under such strict and effective international control as would provide firm assurance that all parties are honoring their obligations. During and after the implementation of general and complete disarmament, the most thorough control should be exercised, the nature and extent of such control depending on the requirements for verification of the disarmament measures being carried out in each stage. To implement control over and inspection of disarmament, an international disarmament organization including all parties to the agreement should be created within the framework of the United Nations. This international disarmament organization and its inspectors should be assured unrestricted access without veto to all places as necessary for the purpose of effective verification."

At the first blush, this sounds like full acceptance of the principle of verification. But the reader should know that the facts actually establish something quite different. The American John J. McCloy had originally suggested the following version of Clause 6: "Such verification should ensure that not only agreed limits and reductions take place, but also that retained armed forces and armaments do not exceed agreed levels at any stage."

The Soviet Deputy Foreign Minister Valerian Zorin had rejected this version in a letter addressed to Mr. McCloy. The Russian agreement was limited to verification of arms destroyed; not to arms in place. Mr. Zorin's letter read, in part: "While strongly advocating effective control over disarmament and wishing to facilitate as much as possible the achievement of agreement on this control, the Soviet Union is at the same time resolutely opposed to the establishment of control over armaments. It appears . . . that the United States is trying to establish control over the armed forces and armaments retained by states at any given stage of disarmament. However, such control, which in fact means control over armaments, would turn into an international system of espionage, which would naturally be unacceptable to any state concerned for its security and the interests of preserving peace throughout the world."

Had Soviet Foreign Minister Andrei A. Gromyko abandoned the Zorin version of verification when he addressed the opening meeting of the eighteen-nation disarmament conference, on March 15, 1962, as follows: "The Soviet Union wishes to have the necessary guarantees that the disarmament obligations that have been agreed upon will be strictly carried out and that there are no loopholes which will permit the clandestine production of aggressive armaments once the process of general and complete disarmament has begun. Our country does not intend to take anyone at his word. . . . Nor do we expect others to take us at our word. The Soviet Union is a firm advocate of strict control over disarmament."

In a Kremlin speech, on July 19, 1963, Chairman Khrushchev offered to exchange inspectors stationed at observation posts at airfields, railroad terminals, highway junctions and ports. In an interview granted to Lord Thomson and reported in the *London Sunday Times* of August 15, 1964, Mr. Khrushchev was asked, "The West thinks any real progress has been held up by Soviet reluctance to allow the principle of free inspection of her own territory. Is there any chance of real progress being made?" He replied, "If we make a disarmament agreement and a start is actually made on disarmament, then we will allow free inspection as part of the specific program—and close inspection, too, so no one cheats."

The Soviet Union has agreed to Article VII of the Antarctic Treaty, Article 13 of the Space Treaty and Article III of the Anti-Proliferation Treaty—all of which provide for inspection.

The Soviet position on inspection is far from crystal clear. But there is reason to hope and believe, based upon these precedents, that the government in the Kremlin might conceivably accept inspection as inseparable from general and complete disarmament.

As was noted above, Secretary of State Frank B. Kellogg offered the traditional response to inspection, on August 18, 1926, claiming that the country "should not be subject to inspection or control by foreign agencies. Limitation must depend on good faith." Inspection is a bugaboo because the concept is approached from a narrow, nationalistic point of view. Thus, every intrusion becomes spying.

The world has been moving away slowly from this extreme position.

For instance, as mentioned above, the Antarctic Treaty

signed by twelve nations, including the Soviet Union and the United States, in 1959, gives signatories the right, under Article VII, to conduct inspections, if they see fit, to satisfy themselves that the "Antartic shall be used for peaceful purposes only." This was the first East-West treaty providing for inspection. Under the terms of this treaty, a team of United States observers actually inspected Soviet stations, during the month of January, 1964, without Russian objection.

On October 1, 1963, the Soviet Union, for the first time, voted in favor of an international inspection of nuclear facilities. The vote came at the seventh annual general conference of the International Atomic Energy Agency at Vienna. The agency's safeguards system, designed to prevent any diversion of nuclear equipment or materials supplied through the agency from peaceful uses to the production of weapons, was extended to large nuclear reactors.

Based on these revised rules, the United States opened to inspection the 175,000 thermal kilowatt reactor of the Yankee Atomic Electric Company in Rowe, Massachusetts. The Agency, thereupon, conducted one announced inspection in November 1964 and two surprise checks in February and April 1965. Three smaller American reactors, two at Brookhaven, Long Island, and one at Piqua, Ohio, had previously been inspected by the international Agency. In April, 1966 the United States offered to open the first nuclear reprocessing plant, in West Valley, New York, to inspection.

In June, 1965, Britain brought its largest nuclear power plant, the Bradwell station in Essex, within the inspection system of the Agency.

A team of 20 inspectors, operating under a budget of

$661,000, goes over the operating books, judges the amount of enriched Uranium in the reactor core, and examines the spent fuel rods that were previously taken from the reactor and placed in water tanks to lose their radioactivity. The purpose is to establish that none of the fissionable material, particularly the Plutonium in the spent fuel rods, is being diverted to the fabrication of atomic weapons. The United States has acknowledged that these safeguards are "practical, unintrusive and effective."

The Agency is expected to increase its inspection force by at least 100 in order to meet its responsibilities under the Anti-Proliferation Treaty.

A 1966 study made by the Washington Center of Foreign Policy Research of the Johns Hopkins School of Advanced International Studies concluded that "A reexamination of the requirements for verification machinery indicates that verification [of production of fissionable materials for atomic weapons] with a reasonable degree of certainty could be achieved through a far smaller organization than any heretofore suggested."

The great hope is that inspection and control in the peaceful uses of the atom would set precedents and examples for inspection and control in the military field. Thus far, Moscow has shown no interest in placing one of its plants under international inspection. But its support of the inspection system is encouraging observers to hope that the Soviet Union will follow the American and British examples, and that of Japan, which has placed her entire atomic energy program under Agency inspection. In all, twenty-seven countries have placed some, or all, of their nuclear power plants under the Agency's system.

Naturally, the Russian repudiation of their previous acceptance of international verification in connection with the test ban treaty has been most disappointing. For three years, from 1958, Moscow was willing to accept fifteen permanent control posts on Soviet territory involving the permanent presence of some 200 foreign observers, and three veto-free inspections a year. The West had even offered to agree that the international inspection teams could be transferred blindfolded to their posts in Soviet aircraft flown by Soviet pilots. Then the Russians backed down. The result is that the Partial Test Ban Treaty of 1963 is only partial and provides for only national detection systems.

The United States has consistently refused to extend the partial test ban to all environments unless this suspension is accompanied by on-site inspection. Thus, on November 25, 1965, United States delegate, William C. Foster, rejected an appeal from thirty-two nations for an unverified suspension of underground nuclear tests as "unacceptable." This stand was taken despite the testimony of Dr. Jerome B. Wiesner that "very nearly all" seismic events of the magnitude that would be regarded as significant in terms of weapons development "would be distinguishable." However the Sterling experiment on December 4, 1966, in a Mississippi salt dome, may have demonstrated that it is possible to decouple some of the shock waves from the surrounding earth by the presence of a dampening air barrier—the "big hole" theory.

The United States also rejected a plan for verification by challenges proposed by Sverker Astrom, Sweden's representative, to break the deadlock between the two major nuclear powers. Mr. Astrom's suggestion was that withdrawal from a comprehensive test ban agreement should be the ultimate sanction against violation. Thus, for example, if Country X suspected Country Y of having staged an underground nuclear test, and Y failed to disprove the charge, X could then withdraw from the agreement. Supposedly, if Y did disprove the charge before a neutral tribunal, it would be awarded a substantial indemnity.

Of course, inspection may also be utilized as an excuse for rejecting disarmament.

Whether authorized by treaty or not, nations have kept other nations under *de facto* surveillance since the dawn of history. Spies have always served a vital function in the scheme of things. With the advance of technology, spy procedures have been refined to the point where each nation has a fairly reliable idea of the state of preparedness of both its friends and its enemies.

The Francis Gary Powers incident, which torpedoed the 1960 Paris summit meeting, publicized the work of the U-2 spy plane. Prior to and since that incident, every square inch of the Soviet Union, Red China, and God knows what other countries has been carefully photographed by United States U-2's and RB-57's. As long ago as April 9, 1956, the United States Senate Committee on Foreign Relations was informed that the flexibility of air reconnaissance was such that ground detail as small as one foot in diameter might be analyzed. A new 2,000-mile-per-hour SR-71 superspy plane is capable of scanning 60,000 square miles of the earth's surface per hour from an altitude of 80,000 feet. Other nations have undoubtedly taken similar steps to secure detailed topographical information. The fact is that we have open skies whether the governments want it or not. The Cuban crisis of fall,

1962 bore testimony to the uncanny accuracy of aerial reconnaissance.

Rocket technology has permitted the major powers to place their spy satellites above the range of existing anti-aircraft missiles. Chairman Khrushchev once hinted in a conversation with an American visitor that his satellites had the United States under observation. The February 24, 1965, issue of *Aviation Week* stated that the Soviet Union had launched fourteen camera payloads in 1964 "under cover of its Cosmos satellite program." This constituted 40 per cent of the thirty-six satellites put into orbit by the U.S.S.R. in that year. During the same year, the United States launched ten (out of a total of sixty-nine) photo reconnaissance satellites.

A whole network of radar installations, sensing devices, and air testing instruments has been installed to detect weapon detonations on and above ground. Progress has also been made in developing seismological stations that can measure underground tremors and explosions.

A world-wide grid of 8,500 observation stations that cooperates with the World Meteorological Organization would be available to assist the proposed United Nations inspection force.

Public opinion has also been moving towards a viewpoint favoring the sort of inspection by the people that would be required to make our proposed treaty work. During March 1958, William M. Evan supervised public opinion polls in six countries for Columbia University to determine the popular attitude on this subject. The actual interviews were conducted by the American Institute of Public Opinion in the United States and by affiliates in other countries. The findings were published under the title, *An International Public Opinion Poll on Disarmament and Inspection by the People: A Study of Attitudes Toward Supranationalism.*

The importance of the results of this study to the validity of the proposals being made in this book justify our reviewing the findings in some detail. The basic questions asked the persons interviewed were worded as follows:

1.) "Would you favor or oppose setting up a worldwide organization which would make sure by regular inspection that no nation, including Russia and the United States, makes atom bombs, hydrogen bombs and missiles?" This was the result of the poll for each country:

Country	Percentage in Favor	Percentage Opposed	No Opinion or No Answer
United States	70	16	14
Great Britain	72	10	18
France	85	6	9
West Germany	92	1	7
India	78	1	21
Japan	91	8	1

2.) "If this inspection organization were set up, would you favor or oppose making it each person's duty to report any attempt to secretly make atom bombs, hydrogen bombs and missiles?" This was the result of the poll for each country on this question:

Country	Percentage in Favor	Percentage Opposed	No Opinion or No Answer
United States	73	11	16
Great Britain	54	15	31
France	74	13	13
West Germany	86	4	10
India	71	2	27
Japan	80	16	4

3.) "If you, yourself, knew that some one in (name of country) was attempting to secretly make forbidden weapons, would you report this to the office of the world wide inspection organization in this country?" This was the result of the poll for each country on this question:

Country	Percentage in Favor	Percentage Opposed	No Opinion or No Answer
United States	80	6	14
Great Britain	50	17	33
France	63	18	19
West Germany	73	11	16
India	63	6	31
Japan	83	5	12

Since the disposition of scientists and engineers to comply with their duty to report violations is of great significance to the question of the feasibility of a disarmament inspection system, it is most interesting to note the percentage in favor. Mr. Evan's survey disclosed that 84 per cent of the scientists and engineers polled would report violations compared to 69 per cent of the non-scientists and non-engineers.

Mr. Evan summarizes his study by stating that the "findings suggest that Inspection by the People is not considered as visionary a proposal as one might have thought."

On September 27, 1960, Chairman Khrushchev stated that he would approve of an arrangement whereby the population of each country would be invited to report violations of a disarmament treaty to an international inspection agency.

13

Inspection by the People

Given the will, it is so laughably simple to accomplish effective inspection and control of a disarmament agreement that the whole thing is almost ludicrous. Since disarmament itself cannot be accomplished unless the people overwhelmingly demand it, it would be up to the people to enforce their disarmament. The people will understand that they possess something priceless in their disarmament treaty. This thing is life itself—their own life and the lives of their children and their children's children. The people will realize that eternal vigilance is the price, not only of liberty, but of life itself. The people will stand eternal guard over their treaty.

The skeptics scoff that the problem of the clandestine nuclear cache itself makes total disarmament especially infeasible. They claim that it would be child's play for a nation to hide 100 bombs completely. Then, if the nations should one day agree to total nuclear disarmament, the critics presume that there would be hiding of nuclear weapons as a hedge against the other side doing so.

Wouldn't it be the counsel of deepest despair to reject the entire idea of general disarmament merely because no foolproof guarantee can be supplied that every ounce of dangerous war material has been accounted for?

The hope lies in the fact that these skeptics are talking about disarmament by the nations which, by their nature, display Machiavellian immorality. The skeptics cannot even conceive of bona fide disarmament by the people. The people are everywhere; they see everything: They fill every interstice and gap and slippage left by the official inspection systems. The Evan poll proves that 50 to 80 per cent of the people are ready to report violations of a disarmament treaty.

A few desperate men, however heavily armed, may cause serious damage, but they cannot stage a military campaign. Nor can they seize control of a society or of a government. For the purposes of widespread evasion of the disarmament treaty, and military action on a meaningful scale, great forces of men are required. The large-scale preparation for war and the concealment of the preparations are social processes involving large numbers of individuals. It is especially easy to inspect the activities of the atomic industry, because production here resembles a great mountain which gives birth to a tiny mouse.

What conspirator would attempt an organized effort to evade a disarmament inspection system when every other person is a possible informer? Even if the proportion who would inform were only one-half of those recorded in favor of inspection by the people, that would still be a source of massive support against clandestine military activities. After all, defection by only one man is necessary to expose any plot.

Each individual in the world, realizing that his own life and the lives of his loved ones are at stake, would become an enforcement officer—a spy for peace. The schools, instead of teaching war and death, would stress peace and life. Armaments would be viewed, not as instruments of glory, but as the unthinkable, unnatural, menacing things they actually are. Thus, millions of additional alert spies for peace, in the persons of our children and our students, would be added to the enforcement army. Who can do a better job of smoking out the hell-holes of war than our children?

The people will feel secure against possible outbreaks of private or collective criminality in the shape of war only when each citizen is a policeman, with the wide world as his precinct. Primary responsibility for enforcement of the people's disarmament must rest on the broad shoulders of the people themselves. That is true security. To put faith in any purely official system of armament inspection is to nourish bureaucratic illusions.

The system of social inspection is particularly valuable in coping with evasions where previously peaceful facilities are converted to military purposes. For instance, to take an extreme case, were the Paris taxis which took General Gallieni's troops to the battle of the Marne civil or military vehicles? Thus, practically any brewery can be turned into a production center for making cholera toxins. Any jet plane can be turned into a bomber. But these facilities do not convert themselves. As long as individuals must do the job, the people will be there—observing. The criminal—as do the people—knows exactly when the warlike intention is put into effect, when the crime is being committed.

Complaint centers, similar to the New York City Box 100, would be set up in various regions by the international inspection force and free communication with these centers would be absolutely guaranteed. The agents of the international force would test the inviolability of the communication guarantee by the simple expedient of dropping unmarked letters in the mailboxes of the world. Citizens volunteering information would be held immune from local police action by provision of the treaty.

Enticing bounties would be offered for informers. At the 1961 Pugwash Conference, Dr. Leo Szilard suggested that, assuming the implementation of a world-wide disarmament, the United Nations might offer a reward of $1 million to informers who turn offenders over to an international tribunal.

Inspection by the people would be supplemented with inspection by the national police forces and by the international inspection force. The latter force would serve under the authority of the United Nations and its activities would not be subject to veto. This force would have absolute freedom of unrestricted access to persons and places, and would carry out inspections anywhere in the world.

At first, the international police force would have to be armed although there should be no necessity to arm it with nuclear weapons. It is hoped that, eventually, in a disarmed world, the international police would have no more reason to carry arms then the London constabulary.

The cumulative disclosures resulting from inspections by the people, the national police and the international police should together reveal any criminal military activities so that flaws in the inspection systems would have to be almost grotesque to permit wholesale evasion. In a multiple inspection system each method would tend to reinforce each other and so insure that the net reliability of the overall system would be far greater than the reliability of any particular method. After all, the amount of control and inspection required for total disarmament is very much less than that required for partial disarmament. The inspectors need not concern themselves over trickles. Since war mobilization is equivalent to a flood, the task of the inspectors would be to watch for floods; and these should not be difficult to detect. The notion of hidden preparations for a major war is absurd.

This does not mean, however, that the United Nations should not take every possible precaution to prevent or detect violations of the disarmament treaty. As mentioned above, a professional international inspection team would be recruited from all the nations of the world, with the proportion from any one country restricted to a small percentage. This force would be well paid, hold tenure, be exempt from all national income taxes, be highly respected, and owe its allegiance solely to the international body.

The activities of the central supranational Authority would be financed by a separate tax levied by the United Nations on international trade. Thus, the Authority would not have to beg, hat in hand, from any nation for its operating funds. The authority would have the power to conduct independent fiscal audits of the revenues, expenditures and budgets of the individual nation-states to ascertain that no moneys were being diverted for military purposes. And each nation would be required to adopt uniform budget procedures to facilitate audits.

Since huge amounts of electric power are necessary for the production of Plutonium and atomic weapons, the inspection agency would have the authority to control the power output of all utilities. To control the production and research of material for chemical and biological warfare, the inspection agency would register, inventory and supervise items of essential laboratory equipment, such as, autoclaves, incinerators, centrifuges, spectrophotometers, fermenters and stills.

The international Authority would have power to license and institute similar controls over the manufacture and transportation of a wide range of critical materials. This list would probably include solid fuels, Uranium, steel, rockets, airplanes, computers, electronic guidance devices, precision gyroscopes, accelerometers, propulsion systems, etc. etc. etc. Light police arms and ammunition would be manufactured by factories operated directly by the Authority.

All atomic power generators would be taken over by the Authority. Isotopes and other nuclear materials for medical and industrial purposes would be purchased directly from the agency and their use would be strictly supervised. Satellites for scientific and communication purposes, such as Telstar, would be launched only by the Authority. That agency would also take over the entire program of moon and space exploration. Uranium mines would be turned over. All international commercial air schedules would have to be filed.

To monitor against possible evasion, the Authority would be equipped with the most modern detection devices, including aerial reconnaissance planes, reconnaissance and Vela satellites, radar installations, seismic arrays, sealed seismic boxes, infra-red spectroscopes, listening devices, and the host of other modern instruments with which this author is not even familiar.

Of course, the Authority is the agency which will have received the census of weapons from the various nations prior to the effective date of the treaty. There should be little concern for concealment of items on this census because the adversary nations should be able to readily supply the missing information from their spy reports. The Authority would also be charged with the most important task of establishing a guard over the abandoned stockpiles of weapons and of destroying the armaments.

As the reader will note, it is our purpose to give the international inspection Authority the widest possible powers to enforce the provisions of the disarmament treaty and to prevent any evasion. It is hoped that the activities of this agency would be conducted according to the strictest principles of democracy, safeguarding the rights and privacies of the citizens. It is hoped that searches and seizures would be authorized in advance by warrants issued by the world courts. It must always be remembered, however, that we are guarding against the greatest scourge that has ever afflicted mankind.

All persons accused of violation of the disarmament treaty would have to be tried either in the national or the world courts. It is hoped that the defendant will receive all the rights of an accused, such as the right to be represented by counsel, speedy trial by jury, the privilege of not being required to testify against himself, the bar against double jeopardy, the right to appeal, and so on. But trial in a national court shall not be a bar to prosecution in the world court. Because of the particularly heinous nature of the crime of accumulating weapons with intent to murder one's fellow men, the punishment set forth in the treaty should be most severe. Perhaps the United Nations would designate certain remote islands as prisons for criminals convicted of violating the disarmament treaty.

It will be noted that the intention here is to treat enforcement, inspection and control as strictly police and judicial functions so as to remove them from the political area completely. The question should be simply, Is the individual charged with violating the disarmament treaty guilty or not guilty as charged?

As we have observed, science and technology are tending to replace industry as the supreme determinants of military capacity, as industry had previously replaced demography and geography. Since the work of scientists and professional engineers is of critical importance for the design and production of modern weaponry, the role and attitude of scientists are crucial to the enforcement of a disarmament treaty. Scientists are thus the key people for implementing and maintaining the disarmament agreement.

True, 84 per cent of the scientists and engineers polled in the Evan survey declared themselves ready to report violations. True, most scientists would agree with the sentiments of Soviet Academician A. A. Blagonravov, as expressed at the 1963 Pugwash conference at Dubrovnik, Yugoslavia: "I am a member of society, that is why I am here. We scientists want to stay alive, the same way as every one else. We have work to do."

Perhaps we need only to appeal to the moral sense of scientists in order to secure cooperation in enforcement of the disarmament treaty. But such a course would be too dangerous. Why should it be assumed that men who had proven themselves so amoral as to create the monstrous murder devices of today are in their right minds or could be trusted?

The safer course would be to require the registration of all scientists and engineers with the international Authority. The central agency would also have to be notified of any changes of employer, position, place of employment or residence. A sudden concentration of such skilled personnel in any one place would, of course, excite suspicion.

Discharged soldiers who had held the rank of officer in the former armed forces would also be required to register and report to the Authority.

This chapter has arrayed a formidable listing of precautions and procedures which might be adopted to enforce a disarmament treaty. No doubt there are any number of other measures which are beyond the knowledge of this author but which can also be brought into play. Inspection by the people, the national police and a United Nations international police force should provide adequate controls to safeguard the treaty.

This does not mean that absolutely foolproof and flawless reliability in inspection for disarmament will be achieved. Perhaps such a degree of perfection can never be attained. But is such perfection necessary for workable control? For instance, the September 1963 Pugwash conference at Dubrovnik, Yugoslavia felt that the possibility of cheating had been greatly exaggerated.

In any event, the risk of evasion by cheating pales into insignificance compared to the risk of a nuclear holocaust.

14

From Here to There

Herman Kahn wrote, "It is the hallmark of the amateur dilettante that he has almost no interest in how to get his particular utopia. Perhaps this is because the practical job of finding a path may be more difficult than the job of designing the goal."

Can we find a path from here—the gathering darkness that forebodes the "final, terrible midnight of mankind" —to there—the bright dawn of world peace? Can we switch mankind from its current collision course with disaster to the broad, bright road of universal brotherhood and peace? Chairman Khrushchev truly stated in his 1964 New Year's message, "Peace is not a New Year gift of Grandfather Frost, it is not a pretty toy that can be plucked from a New Year tree just by reaching out for it with one's hand. Peace must be fought for."

Yes, strangely enough, peace must be fought for to be achieved. To quote Ralph Waldo Emerson, "Peace has its victories but it takes brave men to win them." The times are too precarious to rely on a Micawber optimism that "something will turn up." Or as General Omar N. Bradley put it, "We can't sit about, waiting for some felicitous accident of history that may somehow make the world all right. Time is running against us." There is no doubt but that the law of averages has been more than kind to us. This author, for one, absolutely refuses to be convinced that a system with literally thousands of armed and alert missiles and planes, widely distributed, is actually safe.

Peace will not fly in like a dove or sprout up like an olive branch without the dedicated efforts of human beings. To win the peace, we must wage the peace.

As we have seen, step one in waging the peace is to achieve disarmament. Who is to wage the campaign for disarmament? President Johnson has stated that disarmament is the business of "every parent and teacher, every public servant, every private citizen." These are fine sounding words.

Yet, the parent, teacher, public servant or private citizen who takes these words seriously and attacks the reckless piling of armaments atop of armaments soon finds that he is attacking the very citadel, the heartbeat, of the military-political-industrial Establishment. He will discover that the power elite, entrenched behind its bristling armaments, does not look with benign tolerance upon a troublemaker whose antimilitarism threatens the very mainsprings of power. He will be foully reviled and denounced as a traitor, an enemy of the State, and relentlessly harassed, hounded and persecuted with all the ferocity, cruelty and ruthlessness made possible by the awesome power of constituted government. A government, on the question of armaments, has no opponents—only enemies.

Our leaders act as if the present crazy-quilt nation-state architecture of the world is God-ordained. They take for eternal truth what is only temporary and relative to a particular stage in human history. They retain a warped, self-centered, Ptolemaic picture of the universe. Imagine the irresponsible effrontery of our rulers who, whether self appointed or freely elected, consider it their right and duty to place the interests of the fraction of humanity over which they rule above the interests of mankind as a whole. Imagine the monumental arrogance of our rulers who treat as a purely private right their decisions on matters that will affect the life and health and continued existence of the rest of humanity.

National sovereignty, at one time, served a very necessary function. As its philosopher, Thomas Hobbes, explained it "set before men's eyes the mutual relation between Protection and Obedience." It was the duty of the State to protect the citizen. It was the obligation of the citizen to obey the state. But the compact has become one-sided. The citizen is still expected to render absolute and ultimate loyalty to the national power while that power can no longer deliver on its part of the bargain.

The governments freely admit that they can no longer protect their people in a war. The nations are no longer able to perform their historic role of defender of the lives and properties of their citizens. Walter Bagehot declared that States existed to provide "a calculable future" for their citizens. What State could fulfill that requirement today?

The arms race is, in a sense, a confession of bankruptcy

by the nation-states. They offer no better plan than just fighting and dying until we are all dragged down to eternal destruction and damnation like so many Don Juans. Our rulers lead us in floundering deeper and deeper from morass to quagmire to bog. No one knows how we got into the mess or how to get out of it. All international intercourse has degenerated into the one cliché, "My Pop can lick your Pop."

The introduction of the longbow in the fourteenth century put an end to the role of the armored knight on horseback. The introduction in the fifteenth century of cannons, which could knock down stone walls, put an end to the independence of the local feudal lord in his castle. The king was thus able to establish his supremacy over wide areas and lay the basis for the modern nation-states. The introduction of nuclear weapons in the twentieth century is threatening to knock down the national boundary walls and render obsolete the concept of the self-defensible sovereign state. Certainly, the one thing our weapons cannot do today is to defend the nations and the people who inhabit them.

Our world is in labor. We are confronted with the most frightful human upheaval in the history of mankind. The old order is passing; an age is dying. The ancestral order of power and authority, under which mankind has been accustomed to live, is toppling. Traditional norms which had endured for centuries—even millennia—and acquired sacred connotations are crumbling. Historic values are disappearing, and with them age-old securities. And the people, in their infinite wisdom, sense this foreboding of doom. In the words of Loys Masson, "Now every man is waiting to be shattered! We live in that reign of terror.

Terror lies even in children's eyes. Look at them! Where is yesterday's gleam, like the faint odor of carnations. Night has slipped over it like a cataract, their eyes are blind. . . . Fear is in the eyes of all men, all women; it is a second mother in all mothers!"

In the words of President Johnson, "the forces of the modern world are shaking old ways and uprooting ancient civilizations." Our nation-state system is following the path of decay which had been trod, in earlier times, by such sacrosanct institutions as human sacrifice, slavery, feudalism, laissez-faire, colonialism and the divine right of kings.

The story of the French revolution repeats itself over and over again. The *privilégrés* of the *ancien régime* cannot bring themselves to the point of surrendering their trappings of sovereignty or their special privileges until it is too late. The late Nobel Peace Prize laureate Martin Luther King, Jr. stated, "The old guard in any society resents new methods, for old guards wear the decorations and medals won by waging battle in the accepted manner."

The last place in the world to look for the basic motive power for a supranational control of disarmament is in officialdom. It is completely unreasonable to expect rulers to voluntarily turn in their seals of office and accept lesser roles. The psychology of power and leadership has little margin for subordination. High office would indeed be drab without the pomp and pageantry of the dazzling uniforms, the rows of medals, the tramp of the troops, the saluting of the cannons, the blare of the trumpets.

Wise old Benjamin Franklin once said, "Those who govern, having much business on their hands, do not generally like to take the trouble of considering and carrying into execution new projects. The best public measures are therefore seldom adopted from previous wisdom, but forced by the occasion."

It is never the people who bring war. It is the prideful leader, prating of national honor, trapped by events, thwarted by unfilled visions of glory, thrashing about in ineptitude, who brings war. It is a truism that wars are made by governments and not by people. All people are peace-loving although the regimes under which they live might be aggressors. If we would find the criminal, we must look to the despot who is unable to stand without the support of terror; to the statesman whose hands are bloody through his own incompetence; to the warlord who is calling for a Holy War.

Time and time gain, the people have voted for peace; their elected leaders have given them war. In 1964, the most powerful issue working for President Johnson in the election was peace. When asked to name the stand they would most like to see their party take, Louis Harris reports that Republicans and Democrats alike put "peace working against war" at the head of the list. Yet the harvest again was war.

There is only one great truth for all time. That great truth is that all men are brothers. Our governments have obscured that truth by throwing up Berlin walls which fragment and divide us. It is our leaders who have taught us to distinguish between "they" and "us" in contravention of the great truth that the family of man is one family—"we." There are no superior races. There are no inferior races. There is only one race, which is the great human race.

James Cameron reported in the *New York Times* of December 7, 1965 of a huge mass meeting held in Hanoi, North Vietnam, during the Vietnam War as a "demonstration in favor of the American people." In terming Vietnam, therefore, "truly a looking-glass land," Mr. Cameron misinterprets our great truth. The Vietnamese people are much more perspicacious. Although they may hate Imperialism and Colonialism, they understand that they must love the imperialist and the colonialist simply because they are human. Can the free world, while hating Communism, love the communists?

The Americans will say that Hanoi is full of demons and the Chinese will say it is full of heroes. Perhaps, it is simply that it is full of people, largely indistinguishable from the people of Saigon. South Vietnam and North Vietnam are not homogenous blocks, equally wicked and detestable. They are composites of illiterate peasants, old women and underfed children, as well as besotted officers. It may very well be that the people of North Vietnam are no more the enemies of the people of South Vietnam than the people of South Vietnam are the enemies of the people of North Vietnam. Perhaps it is the leaders—political and military—of both of these countries who are the real enemies of both the South Vietnamese and the North Vietnamese people.

In a larger sense, the people of Hanoi and Saigon are indistinguishable from the people of New York and Moscow and Shanghai. The farmers of North Vietnam, South Vietnam, America, the Soviet Union and China have more in common than in things that separate them. These people are asking for so little. Each wants nothing more than to be left alone, to get on with his work and his life. Each seeks food for his hunger, health for his body, a roof over his head, a chance to learn, a future for his children. Each desires simply to dwell in peace and safety without bullying and fear. Sir Winston Churchill said, "The freedom that matters most today is freedom from fear. Why should all these hard-working families be harassed, first, as in bygone times, by dynastic and religious quarrels, next, by nationalistic ambitions, and, finally, by ideological fanaticism?"

In the stirring words of President Johnson, "We have children to teach, we have sick to be cured, and we have men to be freed. There are poor to be lifted up and there are cities to be built, and there's a world to be helped. . . . It is a crime against mankind that so much courage and so much will and so many dreams must be flung on the fires of war and death. . . . Yet, finally, war is always the same. It is young men dying in the fullness of their promise. It is trying to kill a man that you do not even know well enough to hate. Therefore, to know war is to know that there is still madness in this world."

The death throes of our present nation-state system have caught the peoples of the world in a withering crossfire. Their lands are ravaged, their shops despoiled, their homes burned, their sons conscripted, their children murdered. The entire population of the world is held hostage to horror. A single issue of the *New York Times*, that of February 15, 1966, vividly illustrates the situation. One dispatch relates how pressure mines planted by Vietcong guerrillas on a road near Tuy Hoa blew up three buses filled with farmers, killing fifty-four and wounding eighteen. Another story, filed by Neil Sheehan, relates the "appalling destruction" wrought in Giahuu, South Vietnam, where hundreds of peasant homes were blasted apart by bombs or incinerated by napalm; hundreds of coconut trees, which provide a living for many of the peasants, snapped in half; and hundreds of peasants killed by American artillery and aerial bombardment.

Yes, this is a time for hysteria. This is also a time for lamentation. But, above all, this is a time for thinking. Dr. Samuel Johnson remarked, "Depend upon it, Sir, when a man knows he is to be hanged in a fortnight, it concentrates his mind wonderfully."

Depend upon it, we face a fate infinitely more horrible than hanging and it could overtake us at any moment, much sooner than a fortnight. Man already has one foot in a grave which is an eternity deep.

Socrates once said that the unexamined life is not worth living. Today, it may well be that the unexamined life cannot be lived, but can result only in death. Thomas Jefferson stated, "A country which expects to remain ignorant and free, expects that which never has been and never can be."

The people of both East and West must face the nuclear facts of life. It is understandable that nobody wants to read about the hydrogen bomb, or even to think about it. A Harvard psychiatrist, Dr. Leslie Grinspoon, explains that people "cannot risk being overwhelmed by the anxiety which might accompany a full cognitive and effective grasp of the present world situation and its implications for the future." But, whether one thinks about it or not, the hydrogen bomb will still be there—bigger than life, looming over life. And the more we try to blot out the unthinkable from our minds, the more will it seize dominion over our futures.

The citizens must shrug off the labels, catchwords and slogans, devised by the arts of propaganda, which have become our substitutes for thought. He must reject the arguments addressed largely to the "suspicious, to the backward, to the simple-minded, to the uninformed, to the frightened, and to the timid among us." He must heed the appeal of President Kennedy to "move on from the reassuring repetition of stale phrases to a new, difficult but essential confrontation with reality." Fearful as reality is, it is less fearful than evasions of reality. It is useless to evade reality, because this only makes it more virulent in the end.

The citizen must seize the courage to survey the events of these mean, depressing, brutish and barbaric times. Thousands of rabbits, guinea pigs and other animals have been sacrificed in our laboratories in order to advance the cause of knowledge. Shall we have sacrificed millions of men in our wars and learned nothing? There is a Russian ballad that goes as follows:

> The first war—it's nobody's fault.
> The second war—it's somebody's fault,
> The third war—it's my fault.

Ralph Waldo Emerson said, "We are wiser than we know." We must shut out the noise of the loudmouths, the braggarts, the shouters, the demagogues in our midst. Adlai Stevenson said that the "most important lesson" he had learned was "that in quiet places reason abounds, that in quiet people there is vision and purpose, that many things are revealed to the humble that are hidden from the great." Norman Angell wrote, "In the fundamental problems of human relationship—in those of conscience and morals—the bootblack is as well fitted to judge as the bishop. Indeed, as a matter of simple historic fact (as the political record, for instance, of the Bench of Bishops in the British House of Lords will show) the bootblack has generally been right and the bishop wrong. And this, of course, is because the data for judgment are the common facts of daily life concerning which the bootblack is probably better informed than any bishop could be."

Ponder the message that this book has tried to convey. Ponder the wisdom in the works left behind by the great thinkers. Ponder the history of man. Ponder the writings of the contemporary political philosophers. Ponder the news items carried by the daily newspapers. It is the firm conviction of this writer that such a rational analysis must lead to the conclusions set forth below.

We must conclude with Norman Angell that in that "vitally important field of human activity—the relations between states which are daily becoming more closely concerned with the maintenance of any orderly civilization—we proceed upon assumptions which prove, on examination, to be utterly unsound; often in plain violation of self-evident fact, of common sense, or arithmetic, of any decent workable code of conduct." The world as we perceive it and the world as it really is are two quite different things. We approach twentieth-century problems with thinking that is medieval in many ways. We cling to old myths, illusions and legends.

One of the strongest of these myths is the idea that armaments and the military establishment exist to protect the people. It has never been made clear as to just what the people were being protected from. Could it be that the people were being protected from other people who are their brothers? Is the military guarding the people's democratic way of life? Then it is indeed a strangely secretive, authoritarian, liberty-removing kind of democracy, which tells us to keep our mouths shut and mind our own business.

We must conclude that the mountains of weapons, instead of insuring the security of the peoples, actually pose a most grave menace to that security. Instead of guaranteeing the survival of the peoples, the accumulation of arms imperils that survival. We must conclude that the military exists to preserve the military.

We must conclude that we cannot search for peace through warlike means. Armed forces can wage wars but they cannot make peace because there is the widest of chasms between war and peace. We must conclude that the modern weapons are as obsolete as chain armor in leading us to a solution of the world's many problems. We must realize that all the sense of adventure, glory and heroism has been drained from war. There may have been a remnant of nobility in the willingness to die to the last man. At least the idea was not contemptible. But the willingness to kill the last child can be viewed only as mental derangement. The only way to win an atomic war is to make certain that it never starts. We must put an end to war or war will put an end to us. The ultimate issue, as Boris Pasternak put is, is between civilization and the cudgel.

We must conclude that any society which pins its hopes for survival on its technical ability to massacre millions of the enemy's innocent noncombatants has accepted a degree of moral degradation which denies it any title to being. We must realize that no individual, no nation and no ideology has a monopoly on rightness or on human dignity. It is necessary to reestablish full people-to-people communication and human contact across geographic and political boundaries. We must either learn to live together as a single human family or we must resign ourselves to committing mass suicide.

Deep in our hearts, we must know that our frenzied obsession with armaments is the wrong way to run the world. It contradicts every moral and ethical instinct we have inherited; it violates all our principles as to the dignity and purpose of man. It leaves us with a conscience that is not merely uneasy, but profoundly disturbed.

Faced with the prospect of blasting ourselves and our seed into eternal gibbering night, we must reach the ultimate conclusion that the people—the people and not the statesman—are the primary reality in history. Somehow the whole meaning and purpose of life have been twisted around so that man exists for the State and not the reverse. Man has been transformed into such a collage of official papers—a papier-mâché-human—that we tend to forget the fundamental sovereignty of the individual upon which all government rests.

Ultimately, the fate of the world depends on the individual good judgment of each of us, because the world is made up of individuals. Each individual possesses a claim to the ownership and control of his own life. But, by the same token, man is involved—willingly or not—in the affairs of the world. One cannot withdraw unilaterally from the world to retreat to the private cultivation of one's own suburban garden. Communist or capitalist, black or white, king or pauper, sage or fool, man, woman or child, there will be no innocent bystanders in World War III.

In this crisis, mankind has two alternatives. Like Rodin's statue, we can wrap our arms about our head in a gesture of withdrawal, shutting out sight and sound, and waiting for the inevitable holocaust. We can permit a pall of dull acceptance to settle over our souls. With a melancholy fatalism, we can sink into a miasma of apathy and hopelessness where we no longer care about what will happen to ourselves or to our loved ones. We can continue to act like a Greek chorus that stands at the side watching the tragedy unfold. With Prospero, we can repeat, "And my ending is despair."

The other choice is to stand up and be counted in the crusade against the "fatal foolishness" of armaments and war. The time to take that stand is now, before it is too late, while the last ding-dong of doom is still clanging.

Shall we forfeit by default all mankind's achievements in the arts, science, literature and religion? We cry with U Thant, "Is the human race so destitute of wisdom, so incapable of tolerance, so blind even to the simple dictates of self-preservation that the last proof of its progress is to be the extermination of all life on our small planet? I cannot believe that this is to be the end. I cannot believe that humanity is so bereft of common sense as to launch universal suicide."

If you decline to accept the end of man, if you refuse to die an ignorant death upon a darkling plain, then, you have the obligation—the duty—to rise up against the great evil which threatens us. After all, it is the survival of the peoples of the earth which hangs in the balance; they should have the opportunity to be heard in the matter of the disposition of their lives. They should make their voices heard.

It rests with the individuals to reassert the rule of sanity in opposition to public insanity. The sheer force of unorganized indignation must somehow be channelled into a vehicle for the preservation of human life. Our anguished times cry aloud for some answer but our statesmen stand helpless in the storm. In the same manner that war is too serious an issue to be left to the soldiers, disarmament is too vital to be left to the professionals. The people must dispute the right of a government to obliterate its citizens.

Even as enlightened a statesman as Senator Fulbright states, "The discussion of general and complete disarmament is in my opinion, an exercise in Cold War fantasy, a manifestation of the deception and pretense of the new diplomacy. In a world profoundly divided by ideological conflict and national rivalries—conditions which are almost certain to prevail for the forseeable future—it is inconceivable that the world's foremost antagonists could suddenly and miraculously dispel their animosities and vest in each other the profound trust and confidence which general and complete disarmament would require. There is nothing but mischief in negotiations which no statesman expects to succeed."

Let us, with Nobel Peace Prize laureate Rev. Dominique Georges Pire, react against the false idea that the fate of the world only rests with a handful of politicians whose names appear every day in our newspapers, on our radios and on our television screens. The peace of the world depends upon each one of us. The governments of the world are admittedly bankrupt; it is the obligation of the people to step in as receivers to defend the welfare of mankind.

The citizen will protest his insignificance, his helplessness, in the face of the vast dimensions of the events of this nuclear age. He must be reassured that one man can make a difference and that every man should try. Although man individually may be powerless, collectively the people are the ultimate rulers of the world.

The poet Percy Bysshe Shelley writes:

> Stand ye calm and resolute
> Like a forest close and mute,
> With folded arms and looks which are
> Weapons of unvanquished war . . .
> With folded arms and steady eyes
> And little fear and less surprise,
> Ye are many and they are few.

It is time to translate into reality the dictum of Ernest Bevin that "the common man is the greatest protection against war." Public opinion is a greater power than atomic power. It is the only power which can stop the headlong dash toward obliteration. In the last analysis, there is no civilized nation that can withstand the frown of public opinion.

The forces of evil are in the ascendancy because so many good men have done nothing. It was Baron Montesquieu, the great political scientist, who said, "The tyranny of a prince is not so dangerous to the public welfare as the apathy of a citizen." It must be recognized that the few score officials who now hold power, to our peril, do so through our connivance. These rulers could not, by their physical power, compel hundreds of millions of citizens to go on paying taxes, shedding blood, and taking vast risks year after year.

If we would reduce the war traders to powerless non-entities, we must somehow bring home to the people, whom they exploit, the sense of the futility of armaments and war. We must persuade the people that the taxes paid, the blood shed, the risks taken are quite unnecessary and, indeed, mischievous.

It is with good reason that the people have always held an abiding distrust of authority and politics and their practitioners. Where the nations and their statesmen are dedicated to evil, the burden falls upon the people to restore sanity. If the governments get in the way of the desire of the people for disarmament and peace, these governments will just have to be swept away.

The motive power for the disarmament proposals we have been discussing will have to be supplied by the people themselves. Certainly, they cannot depend on the so-called intellectual leaders who have proved themselves to be the jackals and apologists of the power elite. In the words of Norman Angell, "A decision has to be taken. It has to be taken, not by the experts, the trained economists, the academic specialists, but by the voting millions of over-driven professional men, coal-heavers, dentists, tea shop waitresses, parsons, charwomen, artists, country squires, and chorus girls who make and unmake governments, who do not hesitate, as we have seen, again and again to override the specialist or expert and impose their opinion upon him. With them rests the final verdict."

Francis Bacon said, "By far the greatest obstacle to progress, to the undertaking of new tasks and provinces therein, is found in this—that men despair and think things impossible." So do not despair, gentle citizen. David Riesman has said that "at the very moment when the 'system' appears impregnable to the realist, it often turns out to be vulnerable to the quixotic." There are many imposing monuments to your might, O helpless little people.

It was precisely the little people who brought about the test ban treaty of 1963. We know that our leaders bitterly opposed the cessation of testing in the atmosphere. We remember how the little people who protested this grave menace to its health were harried, beaten and jailed.

Despite the presence of their initials on the document, the Treaty of Moscow had not been negotiated by Averell Harriman, Viscount Hailsham and Andrei Gromyko. A cartoon, appearing in *The Observer* of London gave a more accurate description of the origins of the treaty. The cartoon depicted Britannia knighting a bearded youth wearing ban-the-bomb buttons and the caption read, "Arise, Sir Agitator."

Yes, the test ban treaty had been written by the Aldermaston marchers, by the Women's Strike for Peace pickets at the United Nations, by the Student Peace Union hunger strikers at the White House, by the Committee of 100 sit-downers in Hyde Park, by the Committee for Non-Violent Action paraders in Red Square, by the tormented ghosts of Hiroshima and Nagasaki, by the sailors of the unfortunate *Fortunate Dragon,* by the demonstrators and marchers and protestors in practically every civilized country on earth.

Also, it was precisely the little people who established the principles of civil rights in the teeth of the white power structure. The civil rights legislation was written by the freedom riders, the lunch counter sitters-in, the jail-ins, the department store sit-downers, prayer kneel-ins of the Southern Christian Leadership Conference, the bus boycotters of Montgomery, the marchers of CORE, the demonstrators and protestors who suffered themselves to be kicked, pummelled, bitten by police dogs, drenched by hoses, jailed and murdered.

Every crusade, every beginning of political or social change, must start from small numbers of people convinced of the righteousness of a cause. With Henry Thoreau, we know it well that if one thousand, if one hundred, honest men were actually to withdraw from the co-partnership with existing governments in this most obscene evil of armaments, war and slaughter, it would be the beginning of the abolition of war in the world.

How can the citizen transform his righteous wrath into action? How can he translate the night of possibility into the day of actuality? The method certainly cannot be violent; for violence begets violence and he who takes up the sword will surely perish by the sword. It doesn't make sense, as Serjeant Musgrave learned, to bring in a new war in order to end the old one. A promise of further madness is not a cure for the old madness. President Johnson truly said, "Children cannot learn and men cannot earn their bread and women cannot heal the sick where the night of violence has blotted out the sun." "Not by might but by my spirit," saith the Lord.

The only answer is politics. Aristotle said that man is a political animal. Socrates showed "that all your life, all the time, in everything you do, whatever you are doing, is the time for philosophy. And so also it is of politics." The world is political; we cannot afford to neglect it. Politics has to do with the decisions men make which determine how they shall live and how they shall die.

Political decisions are the ultimate decisions and political science, not mathematics, is the science of sciences.

As John Adams wrote to his wife, "I must study politics and war, that my sons may have liberty to study mathematics and philosophy." Seek ye the political kingdom and all other things will come unto thee. Someone once stated that great issues make great politics. Certainly, there can be no greater issues than war and peace, life and death, annihilation and survival. President Kennedy uttered a truism when he said that "peace is not solely a matter of military or technical problems, it is primarily a problem of politics and people." However, in the great struggle of the twentieth century, of the people against the all-powerful, militarily oriented state apparatus, no one should imagine that existing structures of power will fall like the walls of Jericho at a mere trumpet blast from mobilized world opinion.

It is always difficult to escape from Egypt. Frederick Douglas said in 1857, "The whole history of the progress of human liberty shows that all concessions yet made to her august claims have been born of earnest struggle. If there is no struggle, there is no progress. Those who profess to favor freedom and yet deprecate agitation are men who want crops without ploughing up the ground, they want rain without thunder and lightning. Power concedes nothing without a demand. It never did and it never will. Men may not get all they pay for in this world, but they must certainly pay for all they get. If we are to get free from the oppression and wrongs heaped upon us, we must pay for their removal. We must do this by labor, by suffering, by sacrifice and, if need be, by our lives."

Bertrand Russell enumerated three requirements for

the success of a campaign such as ours. These are, 1.) the enthusiasm of a great moral crusade, 2.) a definite program, 3.) an organization.

1.) certainly, no crusade ever espoused by man ranks with the great cause outlined in this book—that of the survival of mankind. The great moral fervor exhibited and the willingness to sacrifice demonstrated by the members of the Committee of 100, the Women's International League for Peace and Freedom, the Women's International Strike for Peace, the Campaign for Nuclear Disarmament (which sponsors the annual Aldermaston March), the Committee for a Sane Nuclear Policy, the Fellowship of Reconciliation, the Japan Council Against Atomic and Hydrogen Bombs, and other organizations are testimony to the enthusiasm which our crusade generates.

2.) this book outlines a definite program for general and complete disarmament—the first step in the long and arduous campaign to outlaw war.

3.) the form of the organization to spearhead the campaign to achieve disarmament will depend upon the political complexion of the different countries. In the democracies where the instrument of all reform is ultimately the ballot, it should be recognized by now that a reliance upon existing major political parties to effect disarmament courts inevitable betrayal. The major parties are part and parcel of the existing military-political-industrial complex. Their destinies are inextricably intertwined with the lush rewards of honors, profits and position which are spawned by wars and the preparations for war. Only a new political party—a peace party—can mount a meaningful attack on the existing power structures.

The citizen must move into the field of political action

with a new awareness of the great stakes involved. He must form his own political party that will represent *his* interests and he must elect *his* own candidates to office. José Ortega y Gasset wisely observed that "history, like agriculture, draws its nourishment from the valleys, not from the heights, from the average social level and not from men of eminence." A disarmed world will have to be achieved from below; it can never be built from the top down.

Picketing demonstrations, letters to representatives and newspaper advertisements all play a role in man's desperate endeavor to secure a disarmed world. So also is the cause served by *gestes magnifiques*, like those of Abie S. Nathan, Norman R. Morrison and Garry Davis, the Hollywood tower of protest, ballyhoo, individual histrionics and exhibitionism. But like Roman candles, the glow of these *gestes* is so temporary. Instead of isolated deeds of courage, we need concerted grass-roots political action. Lasting, effective political action is only possible through the medium of a people's political party. A party unit should be organized in every locality, hamlet and neighborhood.

The Peace Party should contest every election in the free world at every level. Whether the office be local dog catcher, member of the school board, water commissioner or member of Parliament, the Peace Party should appear on the ballot. During the campaign, and after assuming office, the Peace Party should preach that the number one agenda item for everyone must be disarmament, because unless disarmament is secured, people, dogs, children, schools, water works, parliaments—everything—will go up in flames. There is a world of difference between being represented by officials pledged to your program and elected by your party and writing letters to representatives who must naturally be hostile and who must view your protests with suspicion, as threats to their positions.

The Iron Curtains, Bamboo Curtains, Berlin Walls, barbed wire, and bayonets that partition off the rest of the world shall not suffice to keep from the peoples of the slave world the word of disarmament, peace and brotherhood. Clandestinely and openly, on the streets and in the factories, by word of mouth and by smuggled leaflet, the word shall go out to the oppressed brothers behind the walls. The word shall go out that your brothers on the other side of the curtain have organized for peace, that they are ready to scrap the armaments which threaten you. The word shall go out that your brothers on the other side of the wall are waiting with outstretched hands to embrace you in the name of common, universal brotherhood.

Not even walls or iron bars or chains can withstand the force of concerted public opinion. Liberty is a contagion that cannot be contained. Thomas Paine stated, "An army of principles will penetrate where an army of soldiers cannot. It will succeed where diplomatic management would fail. It will march on the horizon of the world and it will conquer." An idea, such as general and complete disarmament, directed to world sanity and safety cannot be muted indefinitely. Victor Hugo wrote, "More powerful than armies is an idea whose time has come."

If the time has not come *now* for the scrapping of armaments and the outlawry of war, then surely the time will never come. In the short interval before the bombs begin to fall, the message of disarmament must somehow be carried to all the peoples of the earth—carried not on the ends of bayonets but by the force of reason and love.

Soon, underground cells of the Peace Party should begin to appear among the oppressed peoples. With free access to the ballot box barred, the indispensable weapons of political self-determination and self-expression will be the demonstration. The demonstration will be the rite of initiation through which the citizen behind the iron curtain is mustered into the sacred order of freedom. Soon, the peoples on both sides will clasp hands in a common quest for disarmament and survival.

Our campaign is not mainly a negative one, based entirely upon an appeal to fear. The atom bomb has performed its function by shocking the peoples of the world into an awareness of the mortal danger. The bomb may well have been one of the greatest boons ever conferred by science—it may blackmail mankind into disarmament.

Our appeal here is to hope. Our proposals for general and complete disarmament raise a standard to which the wise and the honest can repair. We hold out for mothers the hope that they will not have to bury their torn children. We hold out for the children the hope that they can live out their appointed life spans and achieve the very limit of their capabilities and their desires. We hold out for mankind a chance to live and for future generations a chance to be born. Above all, we hold out a hope that parents, for the first time in a generation, will again be able to look squarely, without guilt and cringing, into the eyes of their children.

We hold out the vision, with Victor Hugo, that "A day will come when a cannon will be exhibited in public museums, just as an instrument of torture is now, and people will be astonished how such a thing could have been."

Index

287